A COMPLETE GUIDE TO BRITISH BUTTERFLIES

Their entire life histories described and illustrated in colour
from photographs taken in their natural surroundings

Margaret Brooks Ph.C., M.P.S., F.R.S.H., F.R.E.S.,
and Charles Knight

JONATHAN CAPE
THIRTY BEDFORD SQUARE LONDON

To my father, John L. Brooks, this work is dedicated. He introduced me to the world of butterflies at an early age, and through the years has given me the benefit of all his own observations and experience. He has produced a never-failing supply of foodplants for our breeding stock, has assisted tirelessly in the fieldwork, has constructively criticized and advised on the photography, and provided the originals for all the drawings and diagrams for this book. Without his active support and encouragement, this work would have been impossible.

M.B.

First published 1982
Reprinted 1983
Copyright © 1982 by Margaret M. Brooks and Charles Knight
Jonathan Cape Ltd, 30 Bedford Square, London WC1

British Library Cataloguing in Publication Data

Brooks, Margaret M.
A complete guide to British butterflies.
1. Butterflies - Great Britain
I. Title   II. Knight, Charles
595.78′9′0941   QL555-G7

ISBN 0-224-01958-9

Typesetting by Rowland Phototypesetting Ltd, Bury St Edmunds, Suffolk
Colour origination by Anglia Reproductions Ltd, Witham, Essex
Printed in Italy by A. Mondadori Editore, Verona

Contents

Acknowledgments   iv
Foreword by David Attenborough   v
Introduction   vii

The Biology of Butterflies   1
  Recognition and Identification   1
  Life Cycle   1
  Anatomy   2
  The Egg   5
  The Caterpillar or Larva   6
  The Pupa or Chrysalis   7
  The Butterfly or Imago   9
  Variation   12
  Enemies and Diseases   13
  Protective Devices   14
  Dispersal and Migration   15
  Nomenclature   16
  Classification   16

Breeding   18

Collecting   22

Photography   25

The Life Histories   28
  Satyridae   30
  Nymphalidae   52
  Nemeobiidae   84
  Lycaenidae   86
  Pieridae   118
  Papilionidae   132
  Hesperiidae   134

Rare Migrants   152

Glossary   157

Index   158

Acknowledgments

My grateful thanks are due to all those friends and acquaintances who have helped so generously in the locating of various species. Without their assistance my task would have been much more difficult and prolonged. I am deeply indebted to the following: Derek Arthurs, Courtenay Banks (who also supplied the photographs of the Black-veined White, the female Brimstone underside, and the Mazarine Blue), Robert Goodden (for permission to photograph the Short-tailed Blue), Philip Grey, Humfrey Halahan, Roy Stockley, Clive Stott, and Dr Jeremy Thomas (who also supplied the photographs of the Large Blue butterfly, larva with ant, and pupa).

We gratefully acknowledge too the contribution made by our publishers, Jonathan Cape Ltd, to the making of this book, in particular to Graham Greene for his sound advice and guidance; to Mary Banks for her understanding and the high standard of her editorial work; to Ian Craig and Alison Lees for the clear and imaginative layout and design; and to Tim Chester for the quality of the production that speaks for itself.

Foreword

Naming creatures is the very basis of natural history. For centuries, the founding fathers of zoology were obsessed with doing so, to the exclusion of almost everything else. And with good reason. Unless you can identify a creature by name, you cannot find out what others have discovered about it, or know whether your own observations are significant or commonplace. But the compulsion to label is not the prerogative of scientists alone. It is felt equally strongly by quite casual observers of the natural world. Many people, fascinated by a strange fossil shape in a stone they have unearthed in a cliff, or haunted by a fleeting vision of a bird, will not rest until they have been able to put a name to it. And many, like me, will want to find out just what butterfly has come into our garden.

You might think that butterflies, of all the wild creatures of our countryside, are among the easiest to identify. Most, after all have brilliant, distinctively marked wings. Nor are there many of them – a mere sixty species (or fifty-nine, if we accept, as sadly it seems we must, that the Large Blue is now extinct in these islands). But that figure gives a misleading impression of the number of different-looking creatures that we may want to name, for of course, every species of butterfly exists in at least four different shapes. As well as a winged adult, we may encounter a species as a chrysalis, a caterpillar or even an egg, and none bears the least resemblance to any of the others. Indeed, these early stages may well be the very ones that we are most anxious to identify, for often our need is not just to pin a label on an adult but to discover what foodplant to provide for a gang of young caterpillars as they clamber out of their eggs, or to predict what kind of winged adult will emerge from a brown anonymous chrysalis.

Yet detailed and accurate pictures of the early stages in a butterfly's life cycle are often very difficult to find. Most field guides to butterflies concentrate almost entirely on the adult forms. This book, on the other hand, not only illustrates every egg, caterpillar and chrysalis of every British species, but even shows the different forms assumed by some caterpillars when they moult. For this reason alone, this book will be enthusiastically welcomed by all of us who are interested in these loveliest of insects.

But there is another reason why this particular guide to British butterflies is of great importance. Anyone who has watched butterflies with any degree of curiosity will, I suspect, have felt an urge to collect them. Capturing a butterfly with the deft sweep of a net, setting each with care, and storing them away in boxes has been a childhood hobby that has led many people to a life-time's interest in natural history. And many a professional entomologist, investigating problems of classification or documenting the ranges of regional variation, has indulged himself by assembling vast collections in which each species is represented by dozens, sometimes hundreds, of nearly identical individuals, immaculately set, arranged in row after regimental row in glass-topped drawers.

Today, however, many of our dwindling populations of butterflies can no longer withstand such wholesale plundering without the risk of extinction. Margaret Brooks, in this magnificent book, has demonstrated a way in which the thrills of collecting and the requirements of science can be continued without damage to the insects themselves – by using a camera. Her superb pictures must provide her, I feel sure, with just as vivid a record of happy and absorbing days in the country pursuing butterflies as any caseful of transfixed bodies. If anyone argues that the taking of a photograph cannot equal, for excitement, a chase with a net, then I suspect that he has never tried to photograph butterflies to the standards so marvellously presented here. And while it is true that some data can only be derived from actual specimens, it is also the case that photographs can yield other kinds of information that dead specimens on pins cannot – such as the nature of the plants on which a species habitually settles, or the precise posture that it adopts to feed or sun itself.

So I welcome this pioneering, new-style butterfly book with delight and enthusiasm, not only on behalf of others who are fascinated by butterflies but on behalf of the butterflies themselves.

DAVID ATTENBOROUGH

Introduction

This book provides a comprehensive guide to the British butterflies, illustrated by photographs of the living insects in their natural surroundings. The sixty different species that breed in the British Isles have been photographed and are described at each of the four stages of their life cycle – the egg, caterpillar, chrysalis and adult butterfly – to show clearly and accurately the distinctive characteristics of their structure, colour and design, so that any specimen found can be readily identified.

All the species which usually breed in the British Isles are included, arranged in their seven families, but the ten species whose spasmodic appearance in our islands causes great excitement in the entomological press are illustrated solely for identification purposes.

There are innumerable variations in many species of butterflies, mostly named by their discoverers, but detailed descriptions of all aberrations do not come within the scope of this book, so only a brief mention is made of variations of each species.

Every species has been illustrated with photographs that show:

(i) the egg taken through a microscope to show clearly its form and colour;

(ii) the caterpillar (larva) as it looks when newly hatched, and after each moult, if any significant changes occur;

(iii) the chrysalis (pupa) in its natural surroundings, showing the method of attachment, and of concealment, if any;

(iv) the adult butterfly, both the male and female when they differ in appearance, together with a picture of the underside of the wings.

The image on the photographs is the image of the living butterfly as it will be found and seen in gardens and in the countryside. A close examination of the photographs reveals details of the anatomy and of pattern and colour that may not be noticed in the wild. As they were taken in the natural surroundings the photographs also contain valuable additional information. They show for instance the foodplant and the type of vegetation the species inhabit as well as the nature and material of any form of tent or shelter they may use, or any hibernaculum or cocoon they may construct.

Some species do not normally rest with their wings open, so the upper surface cannot be photographed in the wild – where this is the case, I have included a photograph of a set specimen for identification purposes. The duration of any stage of a butterfly's life cycle is largely dependent on the weather, so all times given are approximate. As the photographs are not all to the same scale, the average size is given for each stage illustrated.

The need for a guide to butterflies illustrated by photographs of the living insect instead of artist's drawings or dead museum specimens has been apparent to naturalists and entomologists for many years, but this is the first guide of this nature. The use of photographs as illustrations, particularly of the early stages is, I believe, a better means of identification and reference than artist's drawings, as they show more naturally what one is likely to find. All the photographs, except those few for which acknowledgments are made to others, are my own, and were taken wherever possible in the wild. I have also bred, under natural conditions, every species recorded in this book, with the exception of *M. arion*, in order to have each species under constant observation to ascertain and verify the information given.

The book falls quite naturally into two complementary parts. The first part is mainly introductory, and deals with the basic scientific facts of the anatomy and life cycles of butterflies in general. There are also sections on breeding, collecting, and photography. The second section consists of the photographs of each species of British butterfly, together with text giving a description of each stage, times of appearance, types of habitat where it may be found, characteristic and unusual features, foodplants, general distribution in Great Britain, and other information that may be required to find and identify it.

Of all the beauty and wonder of the flora and fauna of the gardens and countryside none is more rewarding to study than the different species of butterflies that can be found in the British Isles. It is an interest that may be pursued at little cost by both students and amateurs alike, wherever they may happen to be. The garden and countryside around one's home are places that contain many beautiful and exciting species, and walks in fields and meadows, on grassy hillsides and embankments, through parks, commons, woods, along wayside verges and hedgerows, and any rough and wild ground bring many exciting discoveries.

Gardens are places where Peacocks, Red Admirals, Small Tortoiseshells, the Whites, and Brimstones may frequently be found, as can certain of the Browns and Blues, depending on the plants grown and the surroundings. The sides of the roads and lanes and any rough or wild land that is met with may be expected to contain their share of interesting species. Grassy hillsides and embankments, chalk downs, and open commons and meadows where the grass has not been cut and where wild flowers grow teem with various Browns, Blues, and with Small Coppers. Woods, particularly of mixed deciduous trees, at their edges and along their paths, clearings and rides have many species of Skippers, Blues, the rarer Hairstreaks and Whites, also the larger Fritillaries, and at times the Purple Emperor and White Admiral. Heaths, moorlands, and open commons are rich in Blues, Green Hairstreaks, Browns and Fritillaries. In whatever part of Britain one may be, and whatever the nature of the surroundings, one may expect to find a quota of beautiful and interesting specimens.

The first butterflies to appear in the year are those that have hibernated since the previous autumn. If the weather is kind the first is seen often as early as February, and is usually the Brimstone. As spring approaches, in March and April Peacocks, Tortoiseshells, Commas, and Holly Blues can be seen, and later Common Blues, Whites, and Orange Tips. With May the season is well under way with Green Hairstreaks, some Blues, Small Coppers, and early Fritillaries. In the summer months from June to September a considerable variety, amongst them the larger Fritillaries, the Purple Emperor, and White Admiral are flying. Early autumn in September and October sees Red Admirals, Small Tortoiseshells and Commas in numbers, particularly in gardens. During November, only a few individuals that are late in hibernating are around. In the winter months the only butterflies seen are those that have been wakened from hibernation by an unusually warm spell.

The most recent detailed study of the life histories of the British butterflies – F. W. Frohawk's *Natural History of British Butterflies*, illustrated with drawings – was published during the 1920s. Since the early years of this century, when his research was done, tremendous changes in the environment have taken place, which have seriously affected our butterflies.

Destruction of habitat is a real threat – the felling of deciduous woodland has hit several species, such as the Purple Emperor and the White Admiral. The Blues, in particular, are affected by the ploughing of downland and old pastures, and by the great reduction in the numbers of rabbits, which formerly kept the turf short by grazing, thereby allowing the butterflies' low growing foodplants to flourish. The use of selective weedkillers, and excessive trimming of roadside verges are especially harmful to the Orange Tip. Dutch elm disease is removing the larval foodplant of the White Letter Hairstreak.

As butterfly habitats and populations dwindle, conservation is of prime importance. Successful conservation cannot be achieved without a detailed knowledge of the species concerned, and such knowledge can be obtained only by careful observation of all aspects of its life history, and the factors governing it. It is my hope that this book may create or reawaken interest in these beautiful and fascinating insects, and in this way help to preserve the butterfly population of these islands.

1981   M.B.

The Biology of Butterflies

Recognition and Identification

There are several features which distinguish butterflies from moths, though the distinctions are not very clear-cut. The most reliable difference is in the antennae – those of butterflies are clubbed at the tip, while those of moths can be of various shapes, none of which ends in a club (Figure 1). Butterflies are therefore referred to as Rhopalocera (club horns), and moths as Heterocera (other horns).

Other general rules are:
(i) Butterflies fly by day, while moths fly by night.
   The exceptions are the Painted Lady, which will fly until after dusk, while some moths (e.g., Burnets) fly by day.
(ii) Butterflies sit with their wings closed vertically over their backs, while moths sit otherwise – either with the wings laid along the body, forewings completely covering the hind, or with the wings held flat.
   The exception to this rule among British butterflies is the Dingy Skipper, which rests like a Noctuid moth.
(iii) Butterflies have no connection between the fore and hindwings, whereas moths have a device (frenulum) which holds the wings together in flight.

The identification of the different species of butterflies relies on differences in internal and external structure. In subdividing the various families, quite small differences in the details of the venation of the wings, genitalia, etc., are significant. The different species of butterflies that are found in Britain are so few in number, only sixty in all, that for general purposes they can quite quickly be recognized on sight, using simply the size, and the colour and pattern of the wings as a guide.

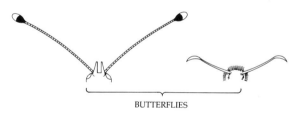
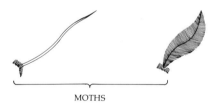

BUTTERFLIES

MOTHS

Figure 1 Shapes of antennae

Life Cycle

Butterflies pass through four distinct stages during their life cycle: (i) egg (ovum, plural ova), (ii) caterpillar (larva, plural larvae), (iii) chrysalis (pupa, plural pupae), (iv) butterfly (imago, plural imagines). The differences in their appearance at each stage are so great that it is hard to believe that one stage can undergo such a complete metamorphosis and develop into the other.

Life starts in the fertilized egg with the formation of the embryonic cell. Fertilization, the fusion of male germ cell (the sperm) with the female germ cell (the egg/ovum), ensures that each individual starts life with a set of genetic material received from both parents, and that in subsequent growth and development it will resemble the species of the parents from which it was derived.

Growth of the embryo occurs by the cell dividing and multiplying in a manner determined by the genetic material inherited from its two parents, and is nourished by the food resources within the egg. When the larva is fully formed it eats its way out of its shell and continues growth and development under conditions entirely different from those experienced within the egg.

The young larva, hatched from the egg at an early stage of development, devotes its life to feeding and growth, stopping only to moult – that is, to shed its skin when it becomes too small and develop a new one that will allow for further growth. The caterpillar stores as much reserve from the food as possible to sustain life through the non-eating pupa stage. When fully grown the caterpillar stops feeding, seeks a suitable place to pupate and moults for the last time, emerging from its old skin into a pupal skin.

Outwardly the pupa appears lifeless but in fact, within is a place of much activity and change. Developments are occurring in its anatomy the complexity of which is little understood. The organs and structure of the crawling, leaf-eating caterpillar are being reconstructed and transformed into a form suited to the needs of the flying, nectar-sipping butterfly. These new organs are being developed for the adult insect from nests of cells (called imaginal buds because they develop into the imago's parts) that have lain dormant in the larva. Certain basic organs of the blood, digestion, senses, and nervous system are reconstructed and adapted for use in the different life form. Organs of the larva that are no longer required undergo dissolution and provide material and energy for the building up of the new organs. The form of the butterfly, and the pattern and colour of the wings, can be seen through the pupal casing a day or two before it emerges.

The function of the butterfly stage is that of reproducing the species, that is, of mating, and in the female of egg production and ovipositing – the laying and dispersal of the fertilized eggs. Food reserves necessary for egg production have been accumulated at the larval stage.

The individual emerges from the egg in a very different form from that of the adult butterfly that it eventually becomes; the changes in form enable the successive stages to lead quite different lives and so reduce the competition there might otherwise be between them. They also enable the species to adapt to the changing conditions of the seasons of the year. Thus its life pattern is in general closely related to the climatic changes of the seasons. Provided the internal development is complete, it is thought to be these climatic conditions – the weather, temperature, humidity, length of day and night – that induce the start of the metamorphosis to a new stage.

The duration of each stage varies according to the species. Some species have only one generation a year, others have two or three. Each species has evolved its own way of surviving the rigours of winter; some do so as eggs, some as larvae, some as pupae, and some as butterflies. The particular stage is constant for each species with one exception, the Speckled Wood, which may hibernate as either larva or pupa. In this book a diagram appears with the illustrations of each species showing the approximate dates on which each stage can be found.

Anatomy

Although the bodily functions which must be performed to support life in a butterfly, as in all insects, are similar to those required in man, the way it achieves them is very different. Both need a skeletal system to support the body; a muscular system for movement; a blood and vascular system to aid and support life-giving processes; a digestive system to provide material and energy to build and operate the body; a respiratory system to convey oxygen from the atmosphere to the tissues, and carbon dioxide resulting from its use back into the atmosphere; a nervous system and sense organs to be aware of what is happening around them and to be able to react in an appropriate manner to external events; and a reproductive system capable of perpetuating the species.

It is worth noting that although considerable changes occur internally at each stage in the development of the butterfly, and that externally the caterpillar, pupa and butterfly are completely different in form and appearance, nevertheless certain vital internal organs such as those that make up the blood, digestive, and nervous systems remain basically very similar in form, and are only slightly modified in the metamorphosis that takes place from one stage to the other. The heart is much the same in all stages; the brain is a lot larger in the butterfly, but the nerve ganglia are very similar; the digestive system that is large and all-important in the caterpillar is smaller and less significant in the imago (Figure 2).

The skeleton of man is internal and the body is formed around it. The skeleton of insects is an outer shell or case made of a non-living material called chitin that is secreted by the outermost cells (the epidermis) of its body, and that dries to form a tough, durable, horny material that encases and protects the delicate tissues of the body and its organs. The larva of a butterfly is divided into thirteen segments that are joined to one another by a flexible fold allowing for movement. Each segment has its own muscles and at points is adapted to form sense organs containing nerves connected to the central nervous system. The abdomen is composed of ten segments, the third to the sixth having a pair of prolegs or false legs which do not survive in the adult butterfly, and the tenth and last segment having a pair of claspers. The body of the adult butterfly is divided into three sections: the head, the thorax, which is made up of three segments – each segment bears a pair of legs but only the second and third bear wings – and the abdomen, which is composed of ten segments.

Muscles are elongated cells enclosed in a sheath of connective tissue, and if stimulated by a nerve impulse will contract, considerably reducing their lengths in doing so. They fall into two groups: the visceral that surround the heart and the alimentary canal and produce the pulsations that move the blood and the food along; and the skeletal muscles that are attached across the joints of the body and of the limbs and appendages, and by contraction and relaxation move one joint on the other. The skeletal muscles are called 'voluntary' muscles because they are controlled and can be contracted at will. The visceral muscles of the heart and alimentary canal are called 'involuntary' as they are not generally controlled in a conscious way.

The blood is not contained within special vessels, but occupies all the spaces within the body, freely bathing all the organs. The circulation of the blood is effected by the pulsations of the long tubular heart which extends the length of the body

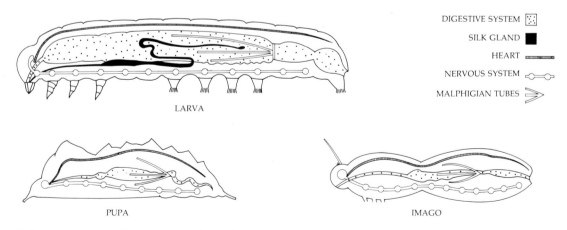

DIGESTIVE SYSTEM

SILK GLAND

HEART

NERVOUS SYSTEM

MALPHIGIAN TUBES

LARVA

PUPA

IMAGO

Figure 2 Internal changes in each stage of development

along the back. Blood is drawn from the body spaces into the heart through minute valves in the wall of the heart, and is pumped forwards and returned to the body to circulate among the various body organs. The chief function of the blood is to carry the necessary nutriments derived from the food to all parts of the body and to collect excretory products. In addition it has an hydraulic function in expanding certain parts of the body to split its chitin casing when moulting and in pumping up the crumpled wings of the butterfly when newly emerged from the chrysalis. It does not act as an oxygen carrier as in man and has very little to do with respiration. It contains no red corpuscles, is a greenish-yellow colour, and is known as haemolymph.

Insects need food to build new tissues and to use as a source of energy. The digestive system consists of an alimentary canal – a tube that runs from the mouth to the anus, consisting of three primary divisions: a foregut, a midgut, and a hindgut. All segments produce a muscular churning movement which serves to mix the content and to carry it along. The foregut serves to conduct the food from the mouth to the midgut. It is in the midgut that the food is digested with the help of enzymes that are secreted there, and where the food is stored until digestion is complete and the nutriments absorbed into the system. The junction of the midgut and the hindgut is connected to the Malphigian tubes, relatively simple glands that extract waste products and impurities from the blood. The waste material of the unused residue of the food and the chemical waste (urine) from the Malphigian tubes pass into the hindgut, and then into the rectum where moisture is extracted and where in the larva the residue is discharged as a pellet through the anus.

Butterflies, larvae and pupae breathe air but as with all other insects have no lungs. Respiration is by means of a branching system of air-tubes called tracheae that conduct air from the atmosphere to all parts of the body. The tracheae are open to the outside air at pores called spiracles that occur on most segments of the body. The tracheae branch repeatedly inside the body, become very fine, and attach themselves to or penetrate the organs of the body. This system provides for the passage of oxygen in the air direct from the atmosphere through the spiracles up the tracheae to the tissues, and for it to diffuse through them to reach the living cells. The waste carbon dioxide is returned in the opposite direction.

It is by means of its sense organs (receptors) in association with an efficient nervous system that an insect, like any other animal, becomes aware of the outside world. Insects are able to react to light, touch, smell, taste, and vibration, but their sense organs operate in a very different way from those of man, and seem to be placed in very odd positions. Vision, differences in light and shade, pattern, colour and movement are of course detected through the eyes, but the eyes are not capable of perceiving as complete an image as the eyes of man. Touch is detected over a large part of the body and legs, where sensitive hairs are connected to nerve fibres that are also sensitive to pressure changes and air movements and so to sound vibrations. Taste is well developed and recognized by receptors in the mouth of the larva and on the feet in butterflies. Smell is the main function of the antennae. Other sense organs spread over the surface of the body react to changes in temperature and humidity.

The central nervous system consists of a double nerve cord, running the whole length of the body under the ventral skin, with enlargements of the nerve cord called ganglia and cross sections in each segment of the body rather like a ladder in shape. The brain, in the head, is the receiving centre of impulses transmitted from the sense organs and is the co-ordinating centre, which as a result of the sensory impulses can send off from certain 'motor' nerve cells impulses to the glands and muscles, causing them to function accordingly. The ganglia consist of nerve cells and form a primitive brain in each segment that enables the various parts of the body to function independently of the brain. A ventral ganglion is the feeding centre and controls the mouth parts, the ganglion in the thorax controls walking and flying, and those in the abdomen control its various functions. None of these centres can start to function of their own accord but must first be stimulated either by an impulse from the main brain or by an outside source.

The reproductive system, apart from the external genitalia, consists of the testes and the ejaculatory duct of the male, and the ovaries and vagina of the female. The ovaries are formed of separate egg tubes. The egg produced by the female will develop only if fused with the spermatozoa cell of the male, and this occurs during egg-laying, not at the time of pairing. After pairing, the male sperm is stored in sperm sacs in the abdomen of the female. When egg-laying is taking place, the male sperm enters the egg through the micropyle as the egg passes the sperm sac on its way down the oviduct. External genitalia vary in form between the different species, and effective contact can occur only when the male and female genitalia fit, so inhibiting breeding between different species. The difference in form, especially of the chitinous parts of the genitalia at the tip of the abdomen, is particularly important in identifying closely related species.

The Egg

When it is laid the egg has a casing of chorion, a protective membrane that forms the hardened eggshell. The fertilized nucleus, the embryo from which the larva will develop, lies embedded in the yolk, a store of food material in the form of protein and fat globules, which provides the nutriment for growth within the egg.

Butterflies' eggs are small, rarely exceeding 1 mm. at the greatest dimension, and are very varied in shape, colour and pattern. They may be fluted, ribbed, pitted, sculptured, or smooth. These details of the egg can be seen quite clearly with a magnifying glass. Each species can be identified by its egg. Those of most of the species in a particular family resemble one another to a certain extent, but there are exceptions. Generally it can be said that the eggs of the Browns are shaped like acorns, those of the Nymphalids similar but with keels, those of the Blues and Hairstreaks like flattened buns with a delicate lacy pattern, those of the Whites and Yellows are bottle shaped, while the Skippers produce a variety of shapes. As this book contains photographs of the eggs of every species, it is only necessary here to show general outlines of the shapes mentioned above (Figure 3).

Every egg has in the top a depression, in the centre of which are several tiny openings, known as the micropyle. It is through these openings that the spermatozoa of the male enter to fertilize the egg as it passes through the oviduct at the time of laying, and air and moisture enter while the larva is developing (Figure 4).

Depending on the species, the eggs may be laid singly or in batches of up to several hundred, attached by a quick-drying sticky secretion to a particular part of a plant. The two exceptions are the Marbled White and the Ringlet, which make no attempt to attach their eggs to anything, but merely drop them amongst grass, which is their

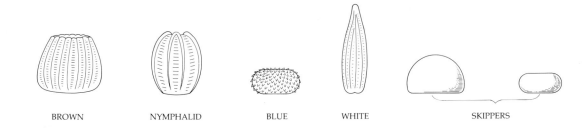

BROWN   NYMPHALID   BLUE   WHITE   SKIPPERS

Figure 3 Examples of butterfly eggs

larval foodplant. Those species which lay their eggs singly usually distribute them over a wide area by laying only one or two on a plant. In most species, the egg changes colour after being laid, and just prior to hatching, the larva becomes visible through the shell.

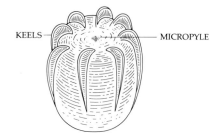

Figure 4 Egg of Large Tortoiseshell

The Caterpillar or Larva

When fully developed, the larva eats a hole in the eggshell – usually in the centre – crawls out, and then, according to the species, may or may not consume the remainder of the shell. In the case of the Speckled Wood, the consumption of the rest of the shell appears to be vital – without it the larva will die.

The larva spends most of its time feeding steadily, an essential occupation, as this is the only stage in a butterfly's life cycle in which growth takes place. The food generally consists of some part of a plant (i.e., leaves, flowers, or developing seeds), although the Large Blue larva in its later stages is solely carnivorous, preying on ant larvae. Each species has its own preferred foodplants, and the larvae will eat only those. The larvae of some species feed only by day, others only by night.

Although the appearance of the larvae of different species varies considerably, they all share the same basic structure (Figure 5).

The larva consists of the head and thirteen segments. The head is made up of two rounded areas, each bearing a group of six simple eyes. Between these groups of eyes is a pair of very short antennae, which are sensory organs to help the larva locate the correct food. On the lower lip are the spinnerets, from which is produced the silk, formed as a liquid by glands in the body. Silk dries very quickly on exposure to air, and is used in a number of ways – to provide a mat on which the larva can rest or walk, and on which it can moult; to act as a lifeline for a young larva if it falls off its foodplant, and as a means of securing and/or concealing the pupa. The head has a pair of strong jaws (mandibles) for biting off pieces of food.

The first three segments behind the head correspond to the thorax of the butterfly, and are called the thoracic segments. Each of these segments bears a pair of horny, jointed legs with claws – the thoracic, or true legs, which correspond to the legs of the butterfly. The larva uses

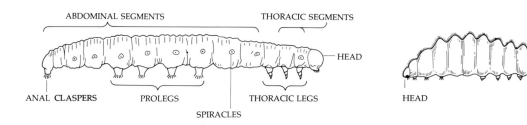

Figure 5 Types of larvae

its thoracic legs for holding the leaf while it feeds. The remaining ten segments are known as the abdominal segments, and four of them bear pairs of fleshy, non-jointed legs – these are the prolegs, or false legs, which form the main means of locomotion for the larva. The feet of the prolegs are equipped with minute hooks which give a good grip, while the centre of the foot acts as a tiny suction cup. The claspers on the last segment are known as anal claspers.

Every segment except the second, third, twelfth, and thirteenth, has a minute opening on each side. These are the spiracles – tiny holes through which air enters and is spread through the interior of the larva by a fine network of tubes.

Some butterfly larvae are adorned with hairs or spines arising from tubercles (warts). Although the spines look sharp, they are usually comparatively soft, and offer no protection against parasites.

Since the skin of a larva forms its external skeleton, it has very limited stretching power, so in order to grow, the larva has to shed its skin several times during its life. This process is known as moulting (ecdysis). As it grows, its skin becomes tighter and tighter, until the larva ceases feeding and settles on a mat of silk for a day or so. It secretes a new liquid skin beneath the old one, then the old skin splits behind the head, and the larva emerges by forcing the old skin towards the tail by muscular action. It then rests for several hours until the new skin has toughened. The interval between moults is known as an instar – thus between emerging from the egg and the first moult, the larva is in its first instar; between the first and second moults it is in the second instar, and so on. The duration of each instar varies according to the species, as does the number of instars – the average number of moults is four. The appearance of a larva changes dramatically between the first instar and the last, sometimes with each moult. The duration of the larval stage also varies with each species; it can be as short as one month, or many months in a species which hibernates as a larva. It can also be shortened or lengthened by temperature variations.

The Pupa or Chrysalis

The general scientific term is pupa; chrysalis – from the Greek meaning gold – refers in particular to those whose skins have splashes of metallic colour, usually gold or silver, on them, as do some of the Fritillaries.

When it is fully grown and in a condition to pupate, the caterpillar stops feeding, thoroughly evacuates the alimentary canal, and seeks a suitable place for pupation. The place selected depends on the habits and needs of the species, but is normally either a foodplant or similar convenient support, or a place to conceal itself if it is to weave a cocoon. From its appearance it is evident that extensive changes have been occurring within the body of the caterpillar. Externally the body appears shorter and fatter, and the colour often changes (Plate I).

The final change into a pupa is similar in its process to that which occurs in previous moults.

The skin around the thorax splits, and by rhythmic contractions the pupa wriggles free. In hanging pupae, this is accomplished thus: when the larval skin has been worked to the tail end, it is gripped firmly between the last two segments of the pupa, while the cremaster (which bears the tail hooks) is withdrawn from inside the skin and quickly worked into the pad of silk, gripping it by means of the tiny hooks.

The pupae of the various species are of three types, named after the three methods of attachment (Figure 6).

(i) **Hanging (Suspensi)**
   The caterpillar spins a small silken pad on a suitable support before pupating, and grips this with its rear claspers, hanging head downwards from the tail end without any other support. The pupa is attached only by its cremaster. (Nymphalidae, most Satyridae)

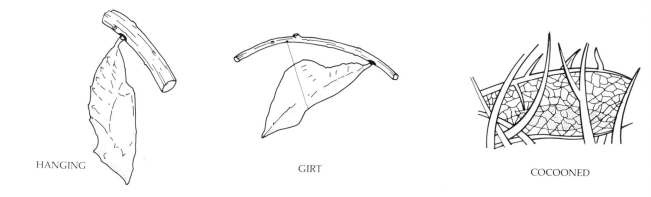

HANGING   GIRT   COCOONED

Figure 6 Types of pupae

(ii) **Girt (Succincti)**
The caterpillar spins a silken pad on a support as do 'hanging' species but in addition spins a girdle of silk which is looped around its thorax and supports it head uppermost. The pupa is attached by its cremaster and the silken girdle. (Nemeobiidae, most Lycaenidae, Pieridae, Papilionidae)

(iii) **Cocooned or Loose (Involuti)**
While none of our British butterflies make a true cocoon, several – mainly Skippers (Hesperiidae) – spin a loose cocoon-like structure amongst the grasses and other plants on which they feed. The pupa may be secured by a silken girdle, or just by its cremaster, or it may be entirely free.

Plate I Pupation of Peacock

When the larval skin has been shed, the pupa emerges pale, soft, and wet, with a covering of chitin. This covering soon dries and hardens, changing shape slightly in the process, and all the appendages and openings other than the spiracles used for breathing are closed and fused to the cuticle. The outward form of the pupal case is clearly shaped to provide for the development and changes that will occur within. In those species which hibernate as a pupa the cuticle that forms the outer case needs to be sufficiently strong and enduring to withstand extremes of weather in exposed conditions. Camouflage is important as a means of protection for pupae. Those of most of the Fritillaries resemble withered leaves sparkling with dew, while that of the Black Hairstreak is uncannily like a bird dropping.

In the pupal stage the insect does not feed and remains more or less motionless, the only movement being a twitching of the abdomen if disturbed. Considerable physical changes take place within to enable the adult butterfly to be formed from the body of the caterpillar. In certain respects this process resembles a second egg stage in which embryonic development is renewed. Cells that have remained dormant in the caterpillar begin to grow and develop to form the organs and tissues of the adult butterfly (wings, reproductive organs, etc.). Some of the vital organs of the caterpillar (of the digestive, blood, and nervous systems) remain and are reconstructed and transformed into the organs of the adult butterfly.

If the upper (dorsal) surface of the pupa is examined, the thorax and abdomen with its ten segments can be clearly recognized. From the sides, and from underneath (the ventral surface) the wings, legs and antennae can be seen neatly placed along each side of the proboscis, which can also be seen lying in a central position along a ventral line. On either side of the head can be seen a large capsule in which the compound eyes of the butterfly will form.

A day or so before the butterfly is ready to emerge, the colours begin to appear in the wings, and can be seen through the casing in which they are enclosed (Plate II).

Plate II Pupa of Large Copper just before emergence

The Butterfly or Imago

When the butterfly is ready to emerge, the skin of the pupa splits behind the head, and by pressing its legs against the inside of the pupa case, it breaks away a portion of the case and squeezes out through the opening thus formed. When newly emerged it is soft and flabby, the abdomen is swollen with liquid, and the wings are small, limp and crumpled. The butterfly then either clings to the pupal case or moves to a position on a stem or other convenient support with its wings hanging down in a limp and wrinkled condition, and starts to pump the fluid from its body into the veins of the wings until they attain their full extent. The butterfly rests motionless with the wings held slightly apart until they have dried and hardened sufficiently for it to fly. The surplus fluid is then discharged (Plate III).

The butterfly has a hard external covering of chitin. The head is comparatively large with much of its space taken up by a pair of compound eyes.

Plate III   Small Tortoiseshell: emergence of the butterfly

The head also bears the antennae and palpi, both sensory organs. A butterfly does not chew and therefore has no mandibles; the proboscis takes the place of the mouth, and this consists of two tube-shaped structures attached to each other in such a way that they form a third tube between them through which the butterfly sucks up nectar and other liquids such as sap from wounded trees, honeydew from aphids, or the juices from rotting fruit. The proboscis is normally kept neatly coiled beneath its head, between the palpi (Figure 7).

The thorax is made up of three segments, although this is not obvious to a casual observer, as they are fused together. Each bears a pair of legs; the second and third segments also bear a pair of wings. The relatively long legs have nine segments, with a hip joint (coxa) at the base; a small segment (the trochanter) movable on the coxa;

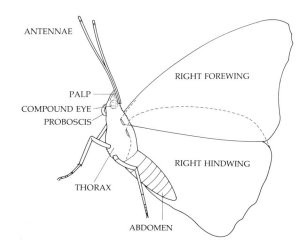

Figure 7 Side view of butterfly (showing wings on one side only)

and three mobile segments, the femur, the tibia, and the tarsus – the last being the foot, which has five jointed segments, the final one ending in two claws (Figure 8). In most species all three pairs of legs are similar, but in the species of two families (Nymphalidae and Satyridae) the first pair of legs is degenerate and useless for walking in that they are small and clawless, so that the butterflies seem to have only two pairs of legs. In some species the feet bear taste organs.

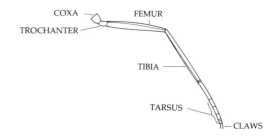

Figure 8 Leg of butterfly

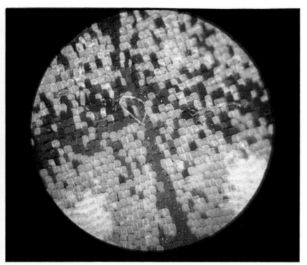

Plate IV Scales on wing of the Peacock

The wings consist of an upper and lower membrane reinforced by a network of veins between them. The scales that cover them are a form of modified hairs. They are like minute flat plates of various shapes, with short stalks which fit in a slot in the wing membrane and overlap each other like tiles on a roof (Plate IV).

The scales are the source of the colour of the wings, and their arrangement forms the pattern and design of their markings. The colour is produced either by a pigment in the scale, or by the ridged structure of the scale itself, which breaks up the light that falls on it, causing changes in colour and intensity according to the angle from which the wing is viewed – as in the case of the male Purple Emperor. The colouring on the underside of the wings is usually much more subdued than that of the upper surface, ensuring that when a butterfly is at rest with its wings closed it

will be far less conspicuous than in flight. The males of many species of butterflies have a number of scales of a different type known as androconia, or scent scales, positioned amongst the ordinary scales, either scattered or in groups. They are attached to a scent gland in the wing membrane from which a scent of a characteristic odour is emitted during courtship to attract the female.

The arrangement of the veins is basically very similar in all species. They are best seen on the underside of the wings. The general pattern of the veins and a system of notation used to identify them (several different systems exist) is shown in Figure 9.

In both pairs of wings is an area clear of veins known as the cell, from which a number of veins

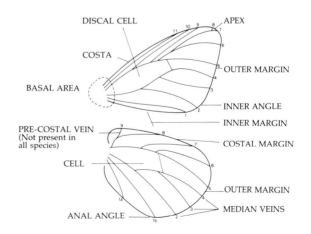

Figure 9 Wing venation of Large White (this species lacks forewing vein 12)

radiate to the outer edges of the wing. For descriptive purposes these veins are numbered from the base of the wing – in the forewing from 1 to 12, and on the hindwing from 1 to 8. The wing surfaces between the veins are called spaces, and are numbered in the same manner as the veins: space 1 lies between the base or inner margin and vein 1, and space 2 between veins 1 and 2. The veins on the edges of the butterfly's wings are named costa (edge nearest thorax), inner margin (bottom or lower edge), outer margin (edge farthest from thorax).

The wings are the first and foremost means of identification of the species of the butterfly. The names given for descriptive purposes to the principal areas of both fore and hindwings as shown in Figure 9 are: basal (nearest to the thorax), discal (middle half nearest to the base), post discal (middle half nearest to the outer edge), sub-margin (surface near the outer edge).

The wings of butterflies have no coupling apparatus, being held together simply by the amount of overlapping of the fore and hindwings.

The abdomen of a butterfly has a thinner covering of chitin than the head and thorax. It is composed of ten segments, but only eight are externally visible, the first two being fused together. The ninth and tenth segments are modified, and form the genitalia concerned with mating and egg-laying. In the female these are fused and contain the vagina into which the sperms are passed and the ovipositor through which the eggs are laid. In the male they contain the claspers – organs to clasp the female – and the penis to eject the sperm. If it is difficult to determine the sex of a butterfly by other features, examine the body from underneath. A female's abdomen is plump, blunt-ended, with the ovipositor showing. On a male the two claspers can be seen, and the abdomen is much thinner.

The butterfly no longer grows or moults. The only change that takes place in this phase of its existence is the maturing of the internal sex organs. Its whole life is orientated towards enabling it to carry out its primary function of mating, reproducing, and the dispersal of its species.

Variation

Specific

In some species, colonies in separate localities differ from each other sufficiently to be classed as a distinct race, or subspecies. This is known as Geographical Variation, and examples are the different races of the Large Heath and the Grayling.

In some of the species which have two generations in a year, individuals of the spring brood are less heavily marked than those of the summer brood, as in the Large White. This is known as Seasonal Dimorphism.

Sexual Dimorphism occurs when the male of a species differs noticeably in appearance from the female of the same species. Examples are the Orange Tip and several of the Blues. In two species only, the Silver Washed Fritillary and the Clouded Yellow, the females alone are dimorphic, having two distinct colour forms.

Individual

Differences in colour or markings in individuals of any species are uncommon, although some species – such as the Chalkhill Blue – are more prone to this type of variation than others. Butterflies exhibiting such variation are referred to as aberrations, and each distinctive aberration which is found is named. Two very extreme and very rare forms of aberration are melanism, an increase in the amount of black pigment present, and albinism, in which the colour becomes very pale or completely white.

Very rarely, specimens occur which exhibit both male and female characteristics of colour and marking – these are termed gynandrous. Where one side is completely male and the other side completely female, the specimen is known as a bilateral gynandromorph (Plate V).

A male with patchy female characteristics, or a female with patchy male characteristics, is known as a sexual mosaic.

Individual variation is normally genetically controlled, but it may be pathological – caused by an injury to the pupa, or by sudden changes in temperature during the late larval or early pupal stages.

Plate V Large Skipper: bilateral gynandromorph (♂ *left*, ♀ *right*)

Enemies and Diseases

The number of eggs laid by the female varies from around forty to many hundreds according to the species, but there is a tremendous loss at all stages of the butterfly's life cycle, and few individuals of a brood survive to adulthood. Considerable losses can occur through unfavourable climatic conditions, as a result of 'bad seasons' for growth and reproduction and for the larval foodplant. Large numbers are taken for food by predators; they suffer loss from disease and infection of various forms, and are subject to decimation by parasites. They are also vulnerable to widespread destruction of their habitat by Man and to his pollution of their environment by chemical weedkillers and insecticides.

Predators
The eggs may be eaten or sucked dry by insects that inhabit the foodplant, particularly those of the Order Hemiptera – the True Bugs – and predatory beetles of the Coccinellidae family, which contains the familiar and brightly coloured Ladybird. Carnivorous slugs, small rodents, and other insectivorous animals will eat the larvae or pupae, and Dragonflies and Spiders prey on the adult butterfly. Birds will consume any stage; tits and other small birds will eat the eggs, and many species will feed on the larvae and pupae as well as on the adult butterfly. A Spotted Flycatcher in the vicinity of a flowering buddleia will take a heavy toll of butterflies visiting the bush.

Parasites
There are two classes of parasites affecting butterflies – parasitic wasps (Hymenoptera) and parasitic flies (Diptera). Some of the wasps (*Trichogramma* sp.) are egg parasites – the female wasp lays her eggs inside the egg of the butterfly, and the larval and pupal stages of the wasp take place inside the butterfly's egg, the adult wasps finally emerging from a hole in the shell. Other species of wasps deposit their eggs in or on a larva. The wasp larvae live inside the body of the host, feeding on blood and fat bodies and avoiding the vital organs. The fully grown parasite larvae then emerge through the skin of the unfortunate host and pupate around or beneath its body. Some species of wasp parasitize pupae, or may not emerge from the host larva until after it has pupated. The flies which parasitize butterflies most commonly are the Tachinidae, which look like bristly house flies; these attack larvae especially (Plate VI).

Diseases
These are many and varied, consisting of fungus diseases, mould caused by damp conditions, and bacterial or virus diseases. They are quite common and usually fatal, and little is known about them. The most frequently seen symptoms are diarrhoea, the body becoming limp, or the steady degeneration of the body into a pool of liquid.

Plate VI   Parasites
(i) Purple Hairstreak: egg with exit hole of wasps (*Trichogramma* sp.)

(ii) Marsh Fritillary: larva with cocoons of parasitic wasp (*Apanteles* sp.)

(iii) Small Tortoiseshell: larva with cocoon of Tachinid fly

Protective Devices

Butterflies

Butterflies in all stages of their development are vulnerable to insect-eating predators and so they have evolved various protective devices and habits of defensive behaviour that contribute to their survival. Adult butterflies on the wing depend for defence against insect-eating birds on swift or erratic flight, and on diverting attention from their vital parts by conspicuous markings and brilliant colours – spots, rings and eyes on the edge of their wings (Peacock, Browns, some species of Blues). At rest most species rely on camouflage: thus some which are brightly coloured on the upper wings have very subdued colours on the underwings, often resembling a part of the foodplant, and are difficult to detect when resting on vegetation or hibernating. Butterflies such as the Comma and Peacock with their wings closed bear a distinct resemblance to dead leaves.

Eggs

Eggs escape the attention of most predators by the smallness of their size, by their basic coloration that often blends with that of the particular part of the plant on which they are laid, or by the position in which they are laid on the plant. They may, according to the species, be hidden on or under flower heads, on the underside of leaves, on the terminal or top shoots of plants, in crevices in the bark of trees, or simply scattered on the ground.

Larvae

Larvae feeding on the leaves of plants are very exposed to attack by birds and other enemies, and for protection rely on either camouflage and concealment or on being unpalatable; while it may appear that spiny larvae have adequate protection against parasites, in fact their armour is useless. Many larvae are well camouflaged: being usually green or brown in colour they merge with the foodplant, an effect that is enhanced by their being marked with lines like the veins of a leaf, or by longitudinal lines to break up their body shape and disguise their presence on a blade of grass. Some species (Skippers) roll leaves; some Fritillaries spin webs to make hideouts or tents in which to live. Others have chemicals in their bodies that make them unpalatable or smell unpleasant, e.g., Large White, and may also have bold colours and markings to serve as a warning to predators. Larvae which are gregarious jerk their heads upwards when alarmed, and may exude an obnoxious fluid from their mouths. The larva of the Swallowtail has a pair of retractile horns (osmeterium) behind its head which it erects when alarmed, and which give off an unpleasant smell. The larvae of many species visit the foodplant only to feed, and at other times conceal themselves away from it.

Pupae

Pupae are normally placed in inconspicuous places and escape attention by camouflage, assuming a colour and form similar to the background. Some pupae, such as that of the Orange Tip, resemble the seed pod of the foodplant, and others – the Red Admiral and the larger Fritillaries – a withered leaf of the foodplant. The pupa of the Black Hairstreak bears a striking similarity to a bird dropping. Skippers (Hesperiidae) spin up cocoons among grasses and other plants on which they feed; others of the large family of Browns (Satyridae) are concealed at the base of the grasses.

Dispersal and Migration

Provided that conditions and the population density of the species remain approximately unchanged, dispersal from an established territory is usually negligible, though spasmodic local dispersals may be caused by changing conditions within the habitat. Shortage of the foodplants owing to overcrowding, or a seasonal failure in the growth of the foodplant may impel the butterflies to travel into neighbouring areas to find suitable plants on which to lay their eggs. Changes in environment owing to temperature, climate and other factors may be a similar influence causing dispersal.

The majority of the species found in Britain are resident populations that are able to maintain themselves as indigenous races. But a few species of British butterflies are found in Britain only as a result of a large scale annual migration to these islands from quite distant places, and they display remarkable powers of flight during the journey. The migration of the adult butterfly from the place of its early stages to localities far distant seems to occur in an instinctive and purposeful manner. The reasons for a migration and the method of navigation employed are not fully understood. A migration could be caused by unfavourable climatic conditions in the usual habitat inducing the individuals to seek better conditions elsewhere, or by a temporary overpopulation of the habitat creating a shortage of the larval foodplants. The species that migrate to these shores fall into four categories:

(i) Species which come every year to reinforce the resident population, and which hibernate and breed successfully, e.g., Large and Small Whites.

(ii) Species which come every year, of which a few individuals may hibernate successfully, e.g., Red Admiral.

(iii) Species which come every year, but which cannot hibernate here, e.g., Painted Lady, Clouded Yellow.

(iv) Species which come rarely, and seldom or never breed here, e.g., Camberwell Beauty, Monarch.

The numbers of migrants which reach the British Isles every year vary considerably, and are believed to be governed to a large extent by weather and environmental conditions prevailing either at the source, or on the route of the migration. The Painted Lady flies northwards from the Atlas Mountains, and other species such as the Red Admiral come from the shores of the Mediterranean countries. There is some evidence of a return migration southwards in the autumn for both these species.

Every so often there is a good 'migrant year', when large numbers of rare migrants are reported here – these are usually helped on their migration by prevailing winds. Examples of such years are 1945, when there was a great invasion of Bath Whites and Long-tailed Blues, and 1947, when countless numbers of Clouded Yellows and Pale Clouded Yellows arrived here.

Nomenclature

All the British butterflies have two names, one English and one scientific; both forms are used throughout this book. The English name is used because it is part of our common language and is therefore the one by which a butterfly is generally known – acquaintance with the English names is in fact all that is necessary to follow a general interest in butterflies. The scientific name is part of an international scientific vocabulary, and is used in a system of classification of all living things according to their physical structure.

Scientific names are based on the Binomial System that was devised by the Swedish naturalist Linnaeus. They have two parts: the first is the generic name – the name of the genus, the group of butterflies similar in form and structure, to which the butterfly belongs. The generic name is a 'Latinized' noun, and is always spelt with a capital letter. The second part is the specific name – the special name of the butterfly that distinguishes it from others within the same genus.

To give the butterfly its full title, the generic name is followed by the specific, and then the name of the first person to describe the butterfly, or by an abbreviation of that person's name, e.g.:

English
Painted Lady

Scientific – Generic
Vanessa

Specific
cardui

Described by
Linnaeus (Linn.)

When a species is variable to the extent that it has definite geographical races, the different races are given sub-specific names. An example is the Silver-studded Blue, *Plebejus argus*. The race occurring on heathland is known as subspecies *argus* (*Plebejus argus argus*), that found on chalk and limestone is ssp. *cretaceus* (larger and brightly coloured), while the smaller race found on the Great Orme is ssp. *caernensis*.

In some cases, the specific name may refer to some feature of the butterfly itself, e.g., *c-album* (the Comma), referring to the white comma-shaped mark on the underside of the hindwing – or to the foodplant of the larva, e.g., *cardui* (the Painted Lady), referring to *carduus* (thistles). Tread cautiously, however, with regard to the Brown Hairstreak, *Thecla betulae*, which has no connection with *betula* (birch).

The English name for a particular species in one country is not necessarily the same as the one used in another country. The butterfly known in Great Britain as the Chequered Skipper, (*Carterocephalus palaemon*), is referred to in North America as the Arctic Skipper, while the butterfly they know as the Checkered Skipper is *Pyrgus communis*, which does not occur in this country. If the scientific names are used, confusion like this will not occur.

Reference to older works on butterflies will soon reveal that several of the scientific names have been changed over the years. This occurs when a group undergoes revision, and either the generic or the specific name (or both) is changed, e.g., the White Letter Hairstreak, *Strymonidia w-album* was formerly *Chattendenia w-album*; and the Silver-studded Blue, *Plebejus argus* was formerly *Lycaena aegon*.

Classification

All animals are classified into groups whose members have the same general construction and the same arrangement of the principal organs, and are significantly different in these respects from other animals. Animals are first of all divided into twenty major groups called Phyla (singular phylum), and then subdivided into Classes, then into Orders, Families, Genera, and finally

Species. Under one of these Phyla, known as Arthropoda (a name that comes from the Greek for jointed) are classified all animals that have a hard external skeleton and jointed limbs. Arthropodean animals are themselves in turn subdivided into four separate classes, each of which, while having the same general features of all arthropods, differs in certain secondary characteristics:

Crustacea – several pairs of legs, two pairs of antennae and no wings: woodlice, crabs, lobsters, shrimps, water fleas;

Arachnida – four pairs of legs, no antennae, no wings: spiders, scorpions, ticks, mites;

Myriapoda – numerous legs, one pair of antennae, no wings: centipedes, millipedes;

Insecta – three pairs of legs, one pair of antennae, three body divisions, mostly winged: butterflies and moths, dragonflies, grasshoppers, wasps and bees, flies, beetles.

Insects as a Class, because of their large numbers, are subdivided into two major sub-classes: the primitive wingless insects called Apterygota, and the more advanced insects that are winged, or have evolved from winged ancestors, called Pterygota. Wing structure is one of the most important features in the classification of Pterygota into twenty-five different Orders, and it is in one of these Orders – that of Lepidoptera (from the Greek *lepis*: scale, *pteron*: wing) that insects with four membranous scale-covered wings, i.e., butterflies and moths, are placed.

Lepidoptera are subdivided into two Sub-orders: Rhopalocera (*rhopalo*: club, *cera*: horn) Lepidoptera with clubbed antennae, i.e., butterflies; and Heterocera (*hetero*: other, different) Lepidoptera with various shaped antennae, i.e., moths, none of whose antennae end in a club.

The classification of butterflies (Rhopalocera) into Families, Genera and Species is based on similarities of wing shape, wing venation, antennae, and genital characteristics. Families are sometimes called Natural Families to emphasize the fact that they are a natural grouping of species that have a number of clearly recognizable features in common. By convention, Family names always end in 'idae'.

British butterflies are grouped into eight differ-

Phylum	Arthropoda	Animals with a hard external skeleton and jointed limbs: insects, crabs, spiders, centipedes
Class	Insecta	Arthropoda with body divided into three sections, three pairs of legs, one pair of antennae: butterflies, moths, wasps, flies, beetles
Sub-class	Pterygota	Winged insects
Order	Lepidoptera	Insects with two pairs of wings covered with scales: butterflies and moths
Sub-order	Rhopalocera	Lepidoptera with clubbed antennae: butterflies
Family	Nymphalidae	Group of butterflies with similar characteristics of wings, antennae, and genitalia: Fritillaries, Vanessids, Purple Emperor, White Admiral
Genus	Vanessa	Red Admiral, Painted Lady
Species	cardui	Painted Lady

ent Families, seven of which are resident and breed here, the eighth – the Danaidae – being a very infrequent visitor from abroad. They are:

Satyridae	Browns
Nymphalidae	Fritillaries, Vanessids, etc.
Nemeobiidae	Duke of Burgundy Fritillary
Lycaenidae	Blues, Coppers, Hairstreaks
Pieridae	Whites, Yellows
Papilionidae	Swallowtail
Hesperiidae	Skippers
Danaidae	Monarch

Families are divided into Genera (singular *genus*: root) that are groupings of closely related species. The name of the Genus, as mentioned under Nomenclature, is part of the scientific name of each species. For example, *Vanessa atalanta* (Red Admiral) and *Vanessa cardui* (Painted Lady) both belong to the Genus *Vanessa*.

Finally we come to the individual type of butterfly – the Species – where all members are identical or very nearly so, and can breed with each other and produce offspring that are similar to each other and their parents in anatomical features, and are themselves fertile.

The table on page 17 demonstrates the steps in the classification of *Vanessa cardui* (Painted Lady).

Breeding

Breeding butterflies is a good way to study each stage of their life cycle, and gives one a sense of satisfaction and achievement. It also provides individuals at all stages of their life cycle in mint condition for photography, and is an excellent way to aid conservation. By protecting the eggs and larvae from parasites and predators a very much greater number of adult butterflies can be produced from a brood reared in captivity than would survive in the wild, and they can be returned to their original home or introduced into a similar habitat that contains their foodplant.

The golden rule for the successful breeding of butterflies is to keep all livestock, at whatever stage it may be, under as natural conditions as possible – in fact create a natural habitat for it. Any attempt to pamper livestock will usually end in failure. Whatever type of housing is used for keeping and breeding butterflies, it is in itself an artificial environment, and this means that special attention must be paid to ensure the normal conditions of air, light, temperature, atmospheric moisture, and food are maintained within the housing; also that there is no overcrowding, and that the environment is sweet and clean.

The life pattern of any stage is closely related to the seasonal changes of climate and length of daylight hours that occur, and the conditions of the relevant seasons must be maintained. The housing must be well ventilated, allowing free circulation of air, and must be such as to admit the normal amount of light and shade, according to the season. The temperature within has a very great effect on growth, which is only possible within certain temperature limits, and must therefore reproduce the normal fluctuations of the day and of the seasons. Care must be taken in placing the housing in a position where it does not become excessively hot in the daytime, and where it is not exposed to too much wind. Moisture requirements are difficult to define accurately, but here again one must be guided by the atmospheric humidity the insect would experience living in natural surroundings. The interior of the housing must never be wet as this will quickly bring mould and fungus disease; neither must it become very dry as then the insect will suffer from water loss which seriously affects its development, and foodplant leaves will shrivel. It is, though, less risky for there to be too little moisture than too much.

Food

A foodplant growing naturally should be used wherever practical. Plants should be potted into containers of a suitable size; clay pots seem better than plastic – some grasses in particular have a tendency to rot in plastic pots. It is important to establish the plants or bushes in the pots some time before the eggs, larvae or butterflies are acquired or you run the risk of the potting being unsuccessful and the plant dying while bearing larvae. When the use of cut rather than growing foodplants is unavoidable there are several important points to remember. Make sure that a continuous supply of fresh cuttings of the foodplant will be available for as long as they are required. Place the cuttings in a jar or similar water container, as one does flowers in a vase, but pack cotton wool around the stems to block the mouth of the container so as to prevent larvae getting into the water and drowning. Foodplants must always be fresh, clean, dry, and free of other insects and predators. Stale or wet plants quickly cause internal troubles resulting in diarrhoea, vomiting, and death. Untiring attention to cleanliness is necessary for successful breeding. Keep a layer of kitchen tissue or something similar on the base of the housing to catch the droppings (frass). Remove this daily and replace with clean tissue. If the frass is allowed to accumulate, it will go mouldy and cause disease. Avoid overcrowding – try to confine yourself to small numbers, particularly of the larger species. This will provide healthier conditions for the larvae and be less of a strain on the breeder. The numbers kept must be determined by the amount of the foodplant available; larvae will consume amazing quantities of food which may need replenishing several times a day if the numbers feeding are not kept in bounds. Always remember that it is both the amount and quality of food supplied that affects growth.

Housing

There is no standard type of cage; anything that will provide a close approximation to a natural habitat can be used. A cage that will give moderate results can be made in a number of ways provided it complies with the basic requirements of air, moisture, temperature, food, and cleanliness outlined previously in this chapter. Wooden cages can be constructed, or an old box converted, provided that at least two sides are covered with fine netting to allow an adequate amount of air and light to enter, and there is sufficient space and height for the foodplants. I do not, however, recommend this form of cage for rearing as it harbours germs and is not easy to keep clean and reasonably disease-free. Neither do I find very suitable cages with plastic covers that are sometimes advocated, as they do not allow sufficient air to flow through and condensation, which is harmful to both larvae and plant, occurs in them readily. As I explained in the Introduction, I have bred fifty-nine of the sixty different species found in the British Isles, and have found from experience the most suitable cages to be those made by fashioning two or more hoops of wire to form a frame which will fit into and over pots or tubs of various sizes and is of sufficient size to give several centimetres' clearance above the foodplant, as shown in Figure 10.

The wire frame is covered with nylon netting with a very fine mesh, to keep out as many parasites as possible. Suitable material may be obtained from an entomological dealer. Secure the

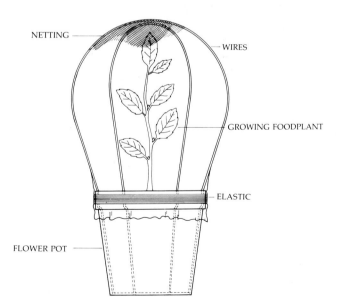

Figure 10 Breeding cage

netting below the rim of the pot with either strong string or strong (1 to 2·5 cm.) elastic. If elastic is used, remember that it has a nasty habit of letting go without warning. Try to avoid folds or pleats in the netting as both butterflies and larvae may become trapped in them.

In rearing butterflies it is necessary to have some knowledge of how they live and what they need at the different stages of their life. Details of the individual life style of each species are given in the life histories section. The following observations are on matters of special concern when breeding butterflies in captivity.

While it is quite possible and sometimes easy to find eggs of a number of species in the wild, the easiest and safest way to obtain them is to capture one or two females together with a male, and cage them with a supply of the foodplant. The odds are that a female captured in the wild will have paired already unless very newly emerged – in this case the male will be necessary. Pairing of butterflies in captivity can be very tricky, as each species seems to require different conditions. Some will pair readily in a small cage over a 12 cm. (5 inch) pot, while others will not perform in anything smaller in size than a greenhouse. The most suitable type of cage for mating butterflies has proved in my experience to be rectangular, with a frame approximately one metre long, 60 cm. high, and half a metre wide, covered with fine netting. Place supplies of the foodplant within the cage, making certain its position will allow the butterflies to fly just over the top. Place as well inside the cage or on the netting one or two pads of cotton wool soaked in a weak solution of honey (one tablespoonful of clear honey in a quarter of a litre of water) to provide nourishment for the butterflies. Alternatively put a small container of fresh flowers inside. Stand the cage in dappled sunlight out of doors; but bear in mind the fact that butterflies fluttering inside a cage have a strange fascination for cats, who will tear the netting to get at them. Protect the pot from rain, and within a few days sufficient eggs should have been deposited, and the butterflies can be released. It will be found that some butterflies will ignore the foodplant and lay their eggs all over the netting.

Eggs

The eggs, unless they have to hibernate through the winter, will normally hatch in a week or two. They should be carefully watched when they begin to change colour, as this is a sign that the young larvae are developing within; when the larvae are ready to emerge, the eggs will darken considerably. Those that hibernate through the winter should be kept in a dry and unheated place – a garden shed is ideal.

Eggs may be collected for breeding, and overwintering eggs on bushes and trees, e.g., those of the Brown Hairstreak on sloe and of the Purple Hairstreak on oak, may be found quite easily during the winter months when the twigs are bare. The twig bearing the eggs should be cut sufficiently long to enable the base to be put into a container of water, and the neck of the container packed with cotton wool. This will prevent the twig from drying out and drawing moisture from the eggs, thus weakening the larvae.

During the flight period, butterflies may be observed in the act of ovipositing. The flight of a female when about to oviposit becomes slow and fluttering, and she hovers over the foodplant, finally settling on it, and testing the leaves with her antennae before depositing.

Larvae

Larvae which are gregarious are the easiest to find, e.g., Small Tortoiseshell and Peacock. Solitary larvae can be found by examining the foodplant for signs of chewing. Bush and tree-feeding species can be 'beaten': hold a beating tray or an open upturned umbrella underneath a branch, and give the branch a smart tap with a stick; the larvae should let go and fall into the tray. An excellent way of collecting Satyrid larvae in the spring is to hold a small plastic box underneath grass which is overhanging the edge of an old anthill, and to riffle through the grass with your fingers – any larvae will fall into the box.

When collecting any stage, be sure that you are not trespassing; if you need to go on to private land, get permission from the owner, otherwise a lot of ill-feeling and unpleasantness may ensue.

While eggs are in general fairly easy to hatch, keeping young larvae alive is a different matter.

This is one of the most critical times in the entire life cycle, and considerable losses occur at this stage, even in the wild. When first hatched the larvae are very small and delicate, and should not be handled unless it is absolutely necessary, and then only with great care, using a clean, dry camel-hair brush. Older and larger ones can be moved by easing them on to a spoon. Larvae must never be left without fresh food; always make sure that there is more of the foodplant than there are larvae to eat it. Never allow them to eat wilted food. When the food supply is getting low, place a container of fresh food beside the old one so that the leaves touch and the larvae can transfer themselves. Larvae sitting motionless and slightly hunched up are probably about to moult. They will change skins four or five times, and to do this will fasten themselves by a silk pad (which is not always visible) to a leaf, stalk, or twig, and they must not be moved at this stage.

The basic requirements for rearing larvae may be summarized as: light and airy conditions within the normal temperature range; absence of condensation and especially wet or dry conditions; ample supply of fresh clean food, and great attention to cleanliness.

Some larvae, such as the Small Blue and the Orange Tip, are cannibals, and individuals should be kept apart. The larvae of some of the Blues need to be in association with ants. This is particularly so in the case of the Brown Argus. If the pot containing the food is standing in the garden, ants will be able to find their way into it. Larvae of a number of species taken in the wild are almost always subject to parasitism.

Pupae

There is no common place or method that larvae use to pupate, and one must be guided by what is known about the pupation sites of the species in nature; these are given in the life histories in this book. Some species will pupate on the leaves or stems, or on twigs of the foodplants, while some may even pupate on the sides of the cage, or at the base. Wherever the site may be within the cage, the pupae are best left where they are. They are fully adapted to living out of doors, so do not try to protect them from the cold and general weather conditions any more than they would be in nature. Those overwintering may be stored in an unheated, fairly dry, and well ventilated place. Cold will not harm them but wet and damp conditions will. Most pupae require a certain degree of moisture when ready to emerge. When the pupa begins to darken just before emergence, a light spraying with rain water can be very beneficial. When the pupae are about to hatch, it is important to ensure that the emerging butterfly has something on which to crawl so that it can dry its wings. It may do this hanging from the roof of the cage, but it is always wise to take the precaution of providing plenty of bare twigs for it to climb up.

All overwintering stock of whatever stage can be kept in suitable containers in a garden shed or outhouse which has a free flow of air through it. Hibernating butterflies such as Peacocks and Commas will settle down quite happily in wooden half-tubs with netting secured over the top with string or elastic. Such butterflies do not pair until several weeks after emerging from hibernation in the spring – when they begin to move, bring the tub outside to a sheltered spot, protect the top from rain, and provide cotton wool pads soaked in honey solution. After a few days of feeding, the butterflies can either be left to pair in their winter habitat, the tub, or they may be transferred to a larger cage.

Collecting

Code for Insect Collecting

The Code for Insect Collecting drawn up by the Joint Committee for the Conservation of British Insects considers that with the ever-increasing loss of habitat, collecting could affect the survival of several species if continued without restraint. It asks all to accept the Code in principle and to try to observe it in practice. It believes that by subscribing to a code collectors will show themselves to be a concerned and responsible body of naturalists who have a positive contribution to make to the cause of conservation. The recommendations that apply generally to the collecting of butterflies are:

No more specimens than are strictly required for any purpose should be killed.

Insects should not be killed if the object is to 'look them over' for aberrations or other purposes. The insects should be examined while alive and then released where they were captured.

The same species should not be taken in numbers year after year from the same locality.

Consideration should be given to photography as an alternative to collecting, particularly in the case of butterflies.

Species listed as endangered should be collected with the greatest restraint – the Committee suggests that a pair of specimens is sufficient – but those species in the greatest danger should not be collected at all.

Specimens of distinct local forms should likewise be collected with restraint.

Breeding from a fertilized female or from a pairing in captivity is preferable to taking a series of specimens in the field.

Never collect more larvae or other livestock than can be supported by the available supply of foodplant.

Unwanted insects that have been reared should be released in the original locality.

The genuine nature lover should make every effort to abide by this code. The destruction of their habitat has reduced a number of our species to a level where any further reduction in the breeding population could be very damaging, the species taking years to build up again, or possibly becoming extinct.

Perfect specimens are best obtained by breeding from a captured female, after which surplus stock can be released to reinforce the wild population.

The conventional collection of dead specimens is nowadays being replaced by collections of coloured photographs of the living insect, and many naturalists find that photographic collections, besides giving a clear and accurate picture of the visual characteristics, also enable them to record the changing aspects of the life cycle that could not otherwise be recorded.

Capture

Before setting out, certain basic equipment is necessary, and can be purchased from an entomological supplier. The most essential item is a net. It is not difficult to make one if the materials are available. The requirements are: a rigid circular or kite-shaped lightweight frame about 30 to 45 cm. across, and a short, preferably detachable, handle a half to one metre long; a bag of black, white, or green cotton or nylon netting of a very small mesh, the length of the bag being at least twice the width so that it may be folded over the frame to prevent the butterfly escaping. The most popular design which can be purchased is known as a kite net, and consists of a nylon net bag on a rigid, usually collapsible frame. A stick or cane may be used as a handle to extend your reach. Spring folding nets are also available, and when not in use can be carried in the pocket or bag. When such a net is folded, it is prudent to keep a stout elastic band round it, as it has a tendency to erect itself inside the pocket or bag at inconvenient moments. Whatever type of net is used, it is essential to carry a spare bag to allow for the disastrous effects of an encounter with brambles.

High speed pursuits across the countryside are rarely necessary to make a capture – a slow, stealthy approach is much more effective. Strike from behind the butterfly if possible – a frontal attack can often be dodged. When the butterfly is in the net, give a quick twist of the wrist to fold the bag over the frame and prevent the insect escaping. A butterfly resting on the ground may be caught by clapping the net over the top of it and lifting the end of the bag – most species will crawl upwards, although some of the Blues do the opposite and disappear amongst the grass.

Flat glass-bottomed inspection jars, or pillboxes as they are often called, are sold by dealers, but can be made quite simply by blacking out the sides and lid of any shallow jar of glass or plastic. Specimens may be removed from the net by carefully placing the inspection jar inside the net and manoeuvring it over the butterfly, which will crawl towards the glass base, enabling the lid to be slid across the top. It can then be examined through the clear base and if unwanted, released again unharmed. Having made sure that the specimen is one that you want, kill it as quickly as possible to prevent any damage to the body, or its scales being rubbed off.

The quickest way of killing a butterfly is by pinching its thorax from below between the thumb and forefinger. This does require practice in order to avoid damaging the specimen. The easiest way for a beginner is to use a killing bottle. This is made from a wide-mouthed screw-cap jar with a tightly fitting lid; into it put on the base a layer of cotton wool dampened with killing fluid – this can be obtained from an entomological supplier. Cover the cotton wool with a sheet of blotting paper. To use the killing bottle, unscrew the cap, insert it into the net and place the neck over the butterfly so that the insect enters the jar, replace the cap, and remove the jar from the net.

Commercially made killing fluid usually consists of ethyl acetate. Strong (880) ammonia can be used, but this affects colours, particularly greens. The traditional killing bottle made up by a chemist always contained potassium cyanide – this is a deadly poison, and should never be used within the reach of children.

Sometimes a butterfly will die 'inside out' – with the wings folded underneath the body. If this happens, gently fold the wings above the body using forceps, while the specimen is still limp.

The specimen having been slain, it can be carried easily by folding it in a 'paper' – a small triangular envelope, many of which can be carried in a small tin or box. Papers can be made of greaseproof paper, or even newspaper, very easily (Figure 11).

Butterflies remain supple for several hours after death, and can be set easily. If kept longer, the whole insect becomes rigid, and must be relaxed before setting is possible. The specimen is placed in a relaxing tin – a flat tin with an absorbent pad on the bottom impregnated with relaxing fluid. It can be improvised by using a plastic box – a sandwich box is ideal. Cover the base with a layer of sand, cotton wool, or polystyrene foam, and dampen with water, or with a commercially produced relaxing fluid. The advantage of using the latter is that it contains a mould inhibitor. Cover the dampened layer with blotting paper, put on this the papers containing the butterflies to be relaxed, and leave in a warm place overnight. Then grip the underside of the thorax below the level of the

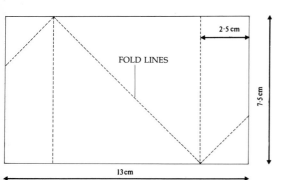

Figure 11 Paper for carrying specimens

wings with entomological forceps (forceps with broad, blunt, curved ends), and exert pressure: this will break the wing muscles, and the butterfly can then be set in the normal manner.

Relaxed specimens are never so easy to set as fresh ones. If possible, always set Skippers when freshly caught, as the wing muscles in this family are very strong, and they are extremely difficult to relax.

Setting

The equipment required is:

(a) *Setting boards* of various widths with a groove running down the centre. The boards can be made of softwood covered with a layer of cork and papered on top (see Figure 12). The boards can be of any convenient length from 15 to 30 cm. or more. The width must be greater than the wing-span of the butterflies to be set, and the groove large enough and deep enough to accommodate the body and legs. To start with, it will be found practical to have at least three boards with the following approximate dimensions:

> For large specimens: width of board 9 cm., width of groove 1 cm., depth 1 cm.
> For medium specimens: width of board 7·5 cm., width of groove 0·75 cm., depth 0·75 cm.
> For small specimens: width of board 5 cm., width of groove 0·35 cm., depth 0·35m cm.

(b) *Setting strips*. These are strips of semi-transparent paper used to secure the wings until the insect has dried out, and may be bought from a dealer. Alternatively, any suitable paper, e.g., tracing paper, may be used.

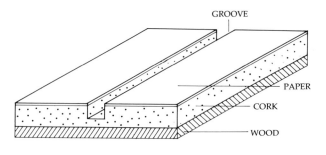

Figure 12 Setting board

(c) *Setting needle*. This consists of a blunt needle fixed into a wooden handle the width of a pencil, and can be improvised quite easily. One can also use a long stout pin, employing the blunt head end to manoeuvre the wings.

(d) *Entomological forceps*. Essential for the handling of specimens, these are curved, blunt, broad-ended forceps (Figure 13).

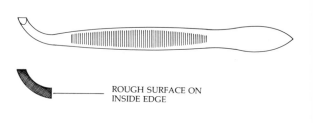

ROUGH SURFACE ON INSIDE EDGE

Figure 13 Entomological forceps

(e) *Pins*. There are two types of stainless steel entomological pins, English and Continental. English pins are of varying thickness and length, whereas the Continental pins are all the same length, but of different thicknesses. Three sizes of English pins will be sufficient to cater for small, medium, and large butterflies. Ordinary household pins should not be used, as they are too clumsy, and will corrode, ruining the specimens.

Select a pin of appropriate size and insert it vertically through the thorax of the butterfly. Then insert the pin in the centre of the groove of the setting board, ensuring that the wings are level on the board (Figure 14). Fix a pin on each side of the abdomen to prevent the body swinging. Using a setting needle, ease the forewing forward by gently pushing with the tip of the needle against one of the larger veins. Raise the wing until the hind margin of the forewing is at right angles to the body. Bring the hindwing forward and then cover with a transparent strip of paper, and secure with pins round the outer edges of the wings, taking care to see that the pins do not pierce the wings. Repeat with the wings on the opposite side of the body. Arrange the antennae, using the setting needle. If the abdomen tends to sag, support it with a small piece of cotton wool, or on two crossed pins. Pin a data label beside the specimen, giving the place and date of capture, the name of the collector, and any other relevant information. Keep the board in a warm, dry, dark place for two to three weeks, until the specimens are dried and may be carefully removed from the board; if removed too soon, the wings will begin to fold up again. Fix the data label on to the pin beneath the butterfly, which can then be placed in the collection. A certain amount of practice is necessary before skill in setting is achieved, so use a common species such as the Large White.

Storage

The ideal home for a collection is an entomological cabinet, but these are so expensive nowadays as to be out of reach of most people, although secondhand bargains may sometimes be found. A cabinet consists of a stout carcass, usually mahogany, containing a number of interchangeable drawers with removable glass lids. Each drawer is lined with cork, papered, and has a camphor cell.

Alternative means of storage are provided by store boxes – each half of the box is lined with cork sheet, and the box usually has a camphor cell. Individual display cases are also available.

Whatever the container, certain conditions are essential. Damp must be avoided at all costs, or the specimens will either go mouldy or 'spring', i.e., the wings will twist or start to close up. The camphor cell must be kept topped up with crushed paradichlorbenzene or naphthalene to discourage the attentions of museum beetles and mites, which will reduce a specimen to a heap of dust if left unchecked.

Every specimen should have the data label on the pin underneath the body. Without such data it will have no scientific value.

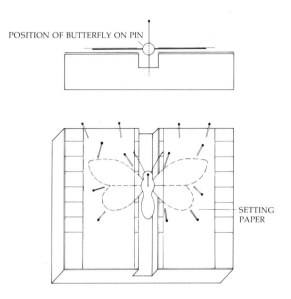

Figure 14 Setting a butterfly

Photography

Photographs of the living butterfly taken in its natural surroundings provide a practical and convenient means of recording the distinctive characteristics of each species. The image on a photograph is the living image, and apart from reproducing the intrinsic beauty of the insect it gives a clear and accurate picture of the anatomical structure, and its colour and markings. When a view of the immediate locality is included, the photograph also provides more general information on habitat, season, etc. Photography is the only practical way by which one can obtain a clear and complete record of all stages of the butterfly's life cycle, and of any significant changes that occur in them – and all stages have a beauty and interest of their own.

General instructions on photography and the operation of the various types of camera are beyond the scope of this book, but can easily be obtained from the many excellent books on photography that are available in bookshops and libraries. This section is concerned with only those matters where the photographing of butterflies makes special demands on the camera or the photographer.

Cameras

The camera used must be one that can be focused on small objects at close range; one with a standard lens will require a supplementary close-up lens or extension tubes to provide in focus a sufficiently large image in relation to the frame. At short focus the depth of field of the lens is also short, and the lens aperture will need to be stopped down to the lower ranges to obtain an adequate depth of field.

The choice of camera and accessories is a matter of cost and personal preference. It is advisable to get a camera that is simple and easy to operate, and also to keep accessories down to the minimum, bearing in mind that it is to be used out of doors, and the equipment will have to be carried over varying distances and in diverse conditions; also that butterflies usually have to be stalked, and that quick action is often needed to get a photograph at all.

A 35 mm. single lens reflex camera is recommended as being the most suitable model to meet all the requirements of butterfly photography. Such a camera can be fitted with all the accessories that may be needed (extension tubes, short focus lens, etc.), it is capable of producing high quality photographs in all likely conditions, it is comparatively light and easy to carry around, and the photographer is able to see through the viewfinder exactly what will appear on the photograph, as problems of parallax are eliminated.

The following different lenses are available:

(i) The standard 50 mm. lens used in conjunction with a set of extension tubes to give a larger image, and to enable the minimum focusing distance to be decreased.

(ii) The standard 50 mm. lens with the addition of supplementary close-up lenses.

(iii) A 50 mm. or 100 mm. Macro lens. This has the great advantage of allowing a subject to be photographed at any distance from 5 to 7 cm. to infinity, and be used with extension tubes to give larger magnifications.

(iv) A Macro-zoom telephoto lens, which is rather heavy and difficult to hold steady in the hand.

Technique

Butterflies are sensitive, nervous creatures, and sudden movement startles them, so a slow, steady approach is necessary. Clothing that is light in colour and shiny in texture should be avoided. A dull colour, preferably green, is good camouflage. Never let your shadow fall over or near the butterfly. The butterfly has frequently to be stalked and the photographer must act quickly to get a photograph. One cannot rely on altering the focusing, light, and distance controls of the camera when close to the butterfly. Thus it is a great help if the controls of the camera are pre-set as accurately as possible so that the camera needs little or no adjustment on the spot. To do this, experiment in focusing the camera on an object of the same size and in similar conditions to those to be found when it's 'for real'. This can best be done in the haunts of the butterfly, using the blossom or foliage of a plant known to be visited by the species. Operate sufficiently near to the subject to give an image that will show details of colour and form, and that usually means as close as you can get to the butterfly without scaring it away.

The shutter speed will be determined by lighting conditions and by the film used, but a useful minimum speed is one-sixtieth of a second. A lens aperture of between f8 and f22 is usually necessary to obtain sufficient depth of field to get the whole subject in focus. With the camera controls pre-set it is possible to creep forward until the butterfly comes into sharp focus. Take care to avoid any movement of the camera when taking the shot.

The use of flash is a matter of personal preference. It is advocated for providing a sharp and brilliant picture in most conditions. Its disadvantages are that as the light conditions are fixed and standard, a rather frozen and unnatural result with a blackish background is obtained, although this may be lessened somewhat by the use of 'fill-in' flash. The subtle gradations of natural light on an object give a more rounded and lifelike picture with no harshness of colour and detail, and in my opinion are infinitely to be preferred.

When photographing butterflies such as the Whites, the Blues, and the Green Hairstreak, it is advisable to under-expose slightly, otherwise halation off the wings will occur. In the case of the Whites, this causes the wings to 'white out', and with the Blues and the Green Hairstreak the colour is lost.

A sturdy tripod will do away with hand-shake, but it tends to be rather impractical for photographing butterflies in the wild because by the time it is set up and the camera focused, the subject is usually miles away.

With so many things to go wrong one must take extra care to get all the camera adjustments right. Wrong focusing, a shutter speed of less than one-thirtieth of a second, and an aperture of lower than f8 is a prescription for failure when photographing adult butterflies. The movement of the camera while taking a shot is a common cause of failure, particularly when the only shot possible is found to be from an awkward and uncomfortable position. As mentioned previously, correct exposure is of prime importance, and when dealing with a small subject, or one which is likely to reflect light strongly, mistakes are easily made even when using a camera equipped with a through-the-lens (T.T.L.) metering system. It is therefore prudent to 'bracket' several exposures, i.e., take one exposure at the aperture you believe to be correct, and then two others, one half a stop above and the other half a stop below the original reading. To improve one's ability it is well worth spending some time practising shots in conditions that are likely to be found in the field.

Films

A good quality high-speed film is most suitable, as this enables you to use fast shutter speeds and small apertures. Such films require accurate exposure, as they usually have little exposure latitude.

Lens Hoods

The use of a lens hood is to be recommended for most shots, but there may be disadvantages – when photographing a very small object at very close range, the subject may disappear into the lens hood before it is close enough to photograph.

Microscopes

By using a microscope, it is possible to see the delicate and beautiful structure of the butterflies' eggs, and the details of the newly hatched larvae. To enable these details to be recorded photographically, several camera manufacturers produce special adapters which permit their cameras to be attached to, and used with, any standard microscope. While eggs are easy to photograph, newly hatched larvae are a different matter; they tend to march repeatedly out of the field of view, demanding great patience of the photographer. One point to remember is that in this type of photography, the depth of field is extremely short, and the subject must be arranged accordingly, e.g., young larvae should be parallel to the film in the camera.

My own methods of obtaining my illustrations for this book were as follows:

All microscope shots were taken using a Kodak Retina Reflex III with microscope attachment.

All other photographs were taken with either

(a) a Kodak Retina Reflex III with supplementary close-up lenses or

(b) a Minolta SRT 303 with 50 mm. Roccor MC Macro lens with or without the addition of extension tubes.

All photographs were taken using natural light, and the film used was mainly Kodak High Speed Ektachrome, with some Agfa CT 18 colour film.

The greatest requisites for successful butterfly photography are patience, perseverance, and good luck – but the satisfaction of obtaining good pictures is worth all the effort involved.

THE LIFE HISTORIES

The seven resident Families of British butterflies are here listed, with their special characteristics. The life histories follow the same Family order with the individual Species being grouped according to Genera, as described on p. 18. (Family sequence varies among different authors.)

For each Species a circular diagram representing the months of the year shows when the different stages of the life cycle occur.

SATYRIDAE (the Browns): *pp. 30–51*

Eleven species.

Four walking legs.

Butterflies predominantly brown in colour, often with pale-centred eye-spots. One or two of the large veins on the forewing are swollen where they join the thorax. Flight usually rather slow and feeble. Found on grassland or in open woodland.

Eggs mostly barrel-shaped.

Larvae feed on grass, and have two conspicuous anal points.

Pupae hanging, cocooned, or loose.

NYMPHALIDAE (the Fritillaries and Others): *pp. 52–83*

Sixteen species.

Four walking legs. Often referred to as the 'brush-footed' butterflies because the forelegs have degenerated into bristly structures that are useless for walking. Wings often brightly coloured, flight usually strong and rapid.

Eggs mostly barrel-shaped, often with longitudinal keels.

Larvae usually spiny.

Pupae hanging, and often adorned with metallic patches.

NEMEOBIIDAE (Duke of Burgundy Fritillary): *pp. 84–5*

One species.

Male has four walking legs, female has six.

Eggs smooth.

Larva woodlouse-shaped.

Pupa bristly.

LYCAENIDAE (Blues, Coppers and Hairstreaks): *pp. 86–117*

Sixteen species.

Six walking legs. In the Blues, males usually more brilliant than females. Hairstreaks have a thin white line on the underside.

Eggs mostly shaped like a flat bun with a lacy pattern.

Larvae woodlouse-shaped with a small head, often hidden under the first segment. Often with a honey gland on the back attractive to ants.

Pupae with characteristic dumpy shape.

PIERIDAE (Whites and Yellows): *pp. 118–31*

Seven species.

Six walking legs.

Upper surface of wings white or yellow.

Eggs bottle-shaped.

Larvae without spines.

Pupae girt.

PAPILIONIDAE (Swallowtail): *pp. 132–3*

One species. Large family, particularly in the tropics.

Six walking legs. Tails on hindwings.

Egg smooth and round.

Larva with retractile horns.

Pupa girt.

HESPERIIDAE (Skippers): *pp. 134–51*

Eight species.

Six walking legs. Heads wide, antennae often hooked.

Swift darting flight. Often rest with forewings partly raised and hindwings horizontal. Found on grassland or in open woodland.

Eggs vary in shape.

Larvae live in tubular dwellings, and are able to catapult their frass some distance in order to keep the dwellings clean, and not betray their presence.

Pupae cocooned.

SATYRIDAE **Speckled Wood**

♀ upper side; wingspan ♂ 47 mm., ♀ 50 mm.

BUTTERFLY
EGG
LARVA
PUPA

Distribution
England and Wales, rarer in the north. In western Scotland and Ireland.

Habitat
Woodland rides and edges, lanes, and hedgerows.

Life cycle
Two generations a year. In favourable years some butterflies may emerge in October/November. Overwinters as either young larvae or as pupae.

Larval foodplants
Grasses, such as couch (*Agropyron repens*), cock's foot (*Dactylis glomerata*), annual meadow (*Poa annua*).

Butterfly
The upper surface is dark brown with straw-yellow spots, some of which contain eye-spots.

The underside of the forewing is similar, but that of the hindwing is a lighter brown with darker markings. Males are smaller and darker than the females, their wings are more pointed, and they have patches of scent scales on the forewings.

Variation occurs mainly in the number and size of the yellowish spots.

The Speckled Wood seems to prefer shade, or at most, dappled sunlight. It takes frequent short flights, resting on leaves or on the ground, and is a frequent visitor to flowers.

Egg
Yellowish-white in colour, with a very finely reticulated surface, the egg is laid singly, usually on a grass blade. It hatches after about ten days.

Larva
Directly after emergence the head is shining black and the ground colour yellowish-white. After the first moult the head and ground colour are green with darker green lines, remaining thus until fully

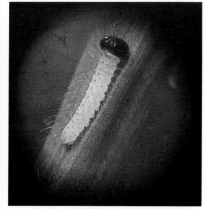

Egg; height 0·8 mm.

Newly hatched larva; length 2·5 mm.

Underside

Fully grown larva; length 27 mm.

Pupa; length 12·5 mm.

grown after the third moult. The anal points are whitish.

The eggshell is eaten on hatching. The larva may feed either by day or night, and this stage lasts about a month, unless the larva is over-wintering, when it lasts about seven months. The Speckled Wood is unique among British but-terflies in that it is the only species which may overwinter in either of two stages – as a young larva or as a pupa.

Pupa

Attached to a pad of silk on a stem, either of the foodplant or some nearby plant. The colour is variable, and may be any shade of green or brownish-green. Those which do not overwinter hatch after three to four weeks.

SATYRIDAE **Wall**

♂ upper side; wingspan 44 mm.   ♀ upper side; wingspan 46 mm.

BUTTERFLY

EGG

LARVA

PUPA

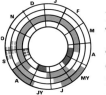

Distribution
England and Wales, Ireland, and south-west Scotland.

Habitat
Hedgerows, hillsides, and grassy areas.

Life cycle
Two generations a year. In favourable years there may be a third generation, producing butterflies in September/October. Overwinters as a young larva.

Larval foodplants
Most of the common grasses.

Butterfly
The ground colour is fulvous (orange-brown), marked with blackish brown, and with white-pupilled eye-spots. On the underside, the forewing is similar but paler, while the hindwing is greyish, marked with dark lines and eye-spots.

Males have a conspicuous band of scent scales on the upper surface of the forewing. Females lack these, are slightly larger, and have more rounded wings.

Variation occurs sometimes in the number and size of the eye-spots.

The Wall is a butterfly which is very active in sunshine. As its name suggests, it will bask on walls and on pathways, and stony banks. It has a restless disposition, and never sits still for long, though it usually remains in a particular territory. It is greatly attracted to flowers.

Egg
The eggs are laid singly on grass blades, usually under an overhang, or in a little hollow in a bank. The colour when newly laid is green, but this changes after a few days to whitish. They have no conspicuous surface features, and hatch in about ten days.

Larva
On emergence, the ground colour of the larva is

♂ underside

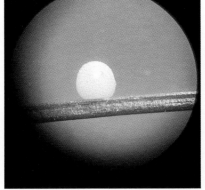

Egg; height 1 mm.

Newly hatched larva; length 2·5 mm.

Fully grown larva; length 25 mm.

Pupa; length 15 mm.

pale ochreous yellow, with a brownish head, and the body is covered with fine hairs. After the first moult the ground colour is green. There are three moults, and when the larva is fully grown the colour is bluish-green with whitish stripes. The anal points are paler green with white tips.

The eggshell is eaten on emergence. The larva feeds mainly at night, and overwintering larvae will feed during the winter months if the weather is mild enough. The duration of the larval stage is just over a month, except for overwintering larvae, in which it is seven to eight months.

Pupa
Hangs from a pad of silk attached to a stem of the foodplant, or of a nearby plant. The colour varies from pale green to almost black, with white or yellowish spots. It hatches after about a fortnight.

SATYRIDAE **Small Mountain Ringlet**

♂ marking on ♀; ♂ wingspan 35–8 mm.

♀ upper side (pale form); wingspan 38 mm.

BUTTERFLY
EGG
LARVA
PUPA

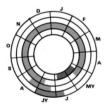

Distribution
Cumberland and Westmorland (Cumbria). In Scotland, Argyll-shire, Inverness-shire, Perthshire.

Habitat
High, often boggy ground, usually over 450 metres above sea level.

Life cycle
One generation a year. Over-winters as a young larva.

Larval foodplants
Mat grass (*Nardus stricta*). In captivity will eat fescues and annual meadow grass.

Butterfly
The ground colour of the upper surface of the wings is dark brown with a reddish band near the outer margin of the wings. This band is broken up into blotches, each with a central black spot. In females this band is sometimes paler in colour than in the male. The antennae are whitish, and the whole body and basal areas of the wings are very hairy. Underside similar to the upper surface, but paler and less distinctly marked.

Variation occurs mainly in the size and colour of the red bands.

The butterflies are active in sunshine, and frequently visit flowers such as tormentil, thyme, dandelion, and hawkbit. The males are very restless, but females fly less, and tend to sit deep in the grass – in flight they look smaller and paler than the males. When ovipositing, the female goes right down to the base of the mat grass.

Egg
Eggs are laid singly on blades or stems near the base of the mat grass, and are at first creamy yellow, with eighteen to twenty longitudinal keels. After about four days the colour becomes paler and blotched with reddish brown, and the egg hatches after about three weeks.

Larva
Directly after emergence, the larva is pale ochreous, marked with brownish lines, and after the

Erebia epiphron (KNOCH)

Underside

Egg, one week old; height 1 mm.

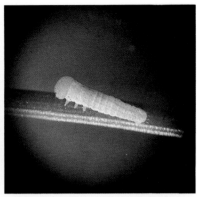

Larva, one day old; length 2 mm.

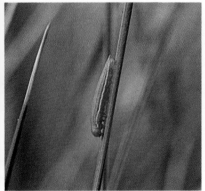

Larva after third moult; length 17 mm.

Fully grown larva; 19 mm.

Pupa; length 11 mm.

first moult it becomes green with whitish lines; this colouring is retained until it is fully grown after the third moult. The anal points are ochreous.

Most of the eggshell is eaten. The young larva hibernates from the end of August until mid-March. Feeding occurs mainly at night, except when fully grown, when it will also feed during the day. It is sluggish in its movements, and feeds on the tips of the mat grass, although when feeding on annual meadow in captivity, it eats notches in the sides of the blades. When about to pupate it wanders about looking for a suitable site. The larval stage lasts nine to ten months.

Pupa

This is formed either on the ground or low down in the grass in a loose cocoon. The colour is green, beautifully marked with brown. The larval skin is not retained, and this stage lasts about three weeks.

♂ upper side; wingspan 45 mm.

♀ upper side; wingspan 50 mm.

BUTTERFLY
EGG
LARVA
PUPA

Distribution
In England, Westmorland (Cumbria). In Scotland, mainly in Perthshire, Argyllshire, Inverness-shire, and Dumfries-shire.

Habitat
Damp areas on hills, usually in open spaces in woods among long grass.

Life cycle
One generation a year. Overwinters as a young larva.

Larval foodplant
Purple moor grass (*Molinia caerulea*).

Butterfly
The upper surface of the wings is dark brown, crossed by reddish bands containing white-pupilled eye-spots. The males are much darker than the females, appearing almost black with deeper red bands, while females have more orange bands with larger white pupils in the eye-spots. The undersides of the hindwings have alternate light and dark bands, which are more pronounced in the female. The undersides of the antennae are white and the legs grey.

Variation occurs mainly in the number and size of the eye-spots, and in the width of the red bands.

The butterfly is restless and difficult to approach, being most active in sunshine, although it will also fly on warm, dull days.

Egg
The eggs are rather large, being just over 1·25 mm. in height, and they are laid singly on the stems or blades of the grass. The surface bears a number of fine longitudinal keels. When first laid, the colour is yellowish-white, but after about five days a pattern of reddish patches develops. The eggs hatch after about a fortnight.

Larva
Directly after emergence, the ground colour is pale ochreous, striped with reddish brown. After the second moult, the colour is pale greenish, and

♂ underside

♀ underside

Egg; height 1·3 mm.

Larva, one day old; length 2·5 mm.

Larva in October, before hibernation; length 6 mm.

Fully grown larva; length 22 mm.

Pupa; length 12·5 mm.

after the third and last moult it becomes pale ochreous with darker stripes, the whole surface being covered with short spines.

Most of the eggshell is eaten on emergence. The larva feeds until October, when it enters into hibernation low down among the grass, usually after the first moult. It hibernates completely until the following March, when feeding recommences. During the day it rests at the bases of the grass stems, coming up to feed only at night. The larval stage lasts about ten months.

Pupa

Ochreous in colour, the pupa is found in a loose cocoon either on the ground, or close to it among the grass stems, and hatches in about a fortnight.

SATYRIDAE **Marbled White**

♀ upper side; wingspan 58 mm.

♂ underside

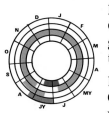

BUTTERFLY ■
EGG ■
LARVA ■
PUPA ■

Distribution
Southern and midland counties of England, and in Yorkshire.

Habitat
Grassy areas such as rough ground, hillsides, downland, and the outskirts of woods.

Life cycle
One generation a year. Overwinters as a first instar larva.

Larval foodplants
Grasses, mainly cat's tail (*Phleum pratense*), cock's foot (*Dactylis glomerata*), and sheep's fescue (*Festuca ovina*).

Butterfly
The ground colour varies from white to cream, with black markings. On the upper surface, the hindwing bears blue-centred eye-spots near the margin. Markings on the underside are similar but paler, with more conspicuous eye-spots. Females are larger and paler than the males, and have browner markings on the underside, particularly on the hindwing.

Variation, which is not frequent, consists mainly of changes in the extent of the black markings.

The flight of the Marbled White is rather slow, and the butterfly frequently visits flowers, particularly thistles, knapweed, and scabious. Colonies can be quite small and localized, the butterfly being found year after year in the same area.

Egg
This is whitish, rounded with a flattened base, and no conspicuous surface features. The female makes no attempt to attach her eggs to anything, but merely scatters them at random amongst the grass, often while in flight. The eggs are laid during July and August, and hatch in about three weeks.

Larva
When newly hatched, the ground colour is pale straw with reddish-brown stripes. There are three

♀ underside　　　　　　　Egg; height 1 mm.　　　　　Larva, one day old; length 3 mm.

Fully grown larva (green form);　Fully grown larva (brown form)　Pupa; length 14 mm.
length 28 mm.

moults, and two distinct colour forms of the larva – in one the ground colour is yellowish-green with darker lines and a brown head, and in the other the ground colour is pale brown with darker lines and a brown head. The anal points are pinkish, and the whole body surface covered with short hairs.

The larva eats its eggshell on emergence, and may take a few nibbles at the grass, but very soon enters into hibernation on a dead grass blade or stem whose colour matches its own. It remains thus until January or February, when feeding begins. It feeds by day, and if disturbed, falls from the grass and rolls into a ring. This stage lasts about ten months.

Pupa
When ready to pupate in June or July, the larva lies on the surface of the ground beneath the grass without any attachment or covering. Over a period of four or five days, it appears to shrivel up, then finally pupates. The pupa is brownish-white with brown markings, and this stage lasts about three weeks.

SATYRIDAE **Grayling**

♂ (*top*) and ♀ upper sides; wingspan ♂ 56 mm., ♀ 61 mm.   Underside

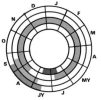

BUTTERFLY
EGG
LARVA
PUPA

Distribution
Throughout the British Isles.

Habitat
Heaths, hillsides, cliffs, and sand dunes.

Life cycle
One generation a year. Over-winters as a young larva.

Larval foodplants
Grasses, mainly couch (*Agropyron repens*), sheep's fescue (*Festuca ovina*), tufted hair (*Deschampsia cespitosa*), early hair (*Aira praecox*).

Butterfly
The upper surface is brown, with ochreous bands which are larger and more noticeable in the female. The male has a dark band of scent scales on the forewing. On the underside, the forewing is orange-brown with white-pupilled black spots, and the hindwing is greyish, marked with black and white. Specimens living in chalk areas tend to have more white on the underside of the hind-wing than those living on heaths, which are darker. There are several subspecies, among them *scota* from eastern Scotland – brightly marked, more orange; *hibernica* from Ireland – brightly marked, more reddish; *clarensis* from Co. Clare and Co. Galway – greyer underside; *thyone* from Great Orme – smaller, flies in late June.

Variation can occur in the number and size of the 'eyes'.

The flight is swift but short, and as soon as the butterfly settles on the ground, it closes its wings, lowering the forewings between the hind pair, and tilts over, seemingly to avoid casting a shadow. The perfect blending of the hindwings with their surroundings provides incredibly good camouflage. During courtship, the male settles in front of the female and flutters his wings very rapidly.

Egg
Laid singly on grass stems or blades from July to September, the eggs are white in colour, with about twenty-eight longitudinal ribs. They hatch in about two and a half weeks.

Egg; height 0·8 mm.

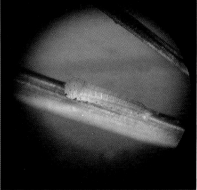
Larva, one day old; length 1·5 mm.

Larva before second moult; length 7 mm.

Fully grown larva; length 30 mm.

Pupa; length 16 mm.

Larva

Newly emerged, the larva is cream-coloured with brownish lines. After the first moult, the colour is ochreous with brown and white lines. There are four moults, and when fully grown, the larva is yellowish-white with brown and white stripes, and with ochreous anal points. It hibernates after the second moult, low down among the grass, although it will feed during mild weather in the winter. It feeds at night, resting low down among the grass during the day. The larval stage lasts nine to ten months.

Pupa

The pupa is rich reddish-brown, and is formed in a chamber just below the surface of the soil, where it rests without any attachment, hatching after about a month.

SATYRIDAE **Meadow Brown**

♂ upper side; wingspan 50 mm.

♀ upper side; wingspan 55 mm.

BUTTERFLY

EGG

LARVA

PUPA

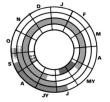

Distribution
Throughout the British Isles.

Habitat
Almost any grassy area, e.g., hillsides, fields, open areas in woods, roadside verges.

Life cycle
One generation a year, possibly two; in favourable years, fresh specimens may be seen in the autumn. Overwinters as a young larva.

Larval foodplants
Grasses, especially *Poa* spp.

Butterfly
The sexes are so different in appearance that they were described originally as separate species. The upper side of the male is dark brown. The forewing has a black band of scent scales and a white-pupilled black eye-spot near the apex, often with a small orange patch below it. On the underside, the forewing is orange with a greyish-brown border the same colour as the hindwings. Females are larger, the upper side has much more orange, and lacks the scent scales. The underside of the hindwing has a paler band. There are several subspecies; the typical one is known as *insularis*. Others are: *splendida* from western Scotland and the Hebrides – large, bright, with a darker ground colour; *iernes* from Ireland – bright, with a more uniform underside; *cassiteridum* from the Scilly Isles – small, with a mottled underside.

There is considerable variation in the eye-spots and the amount of orange. In some specimens the orange is replaced by white.

Probably our commonest butterfly, the Meadow Brown may be found on the wing from late June to September. It seems admirably suited to the British climate, since it will fly even in the dullest weather. It is a frequent visitor to flowers, particularly thistles and knapweeds.

Egg
Eggs are laid singly, usually on dead grass blades, and are small in comparison to the size of the

Maniola jurtina (LINNAEUS)

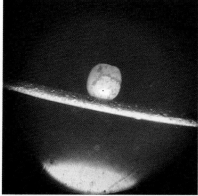

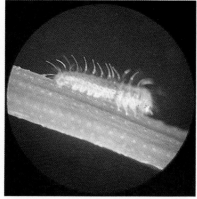

Undersides: ♀ *above*, ♂ *below*

Egg; height 0·5 mm.

Larva, one day old; length 1·4 mm.

Larva after fourth moult; length 10 mm.

Fully grown larva; length 25 mm.

Pupa; length 15·5 mm.

butterfly. They are flat-topped, with about twenty-four longitudinal keels, and when first laid are yellowish-white in colour, but after about a week the surface becomes covered with reddish blotches. They hatch after about three weeks.

Larva

When newly emerged, the larva is ochreous with reddish-brown lines, the ground colour becoming greenish when feeding commences. After the first moult, the colour is green with darker green and white lines, this colouring remaining the same until the larva is fully grown, after the fifth moult. The whole body is covered with whitish hairs, and the anal points are white.

There is only a partial hibernation, low down among the grass, the larva coming out to feed during mild winter weather. Feeding takes place mainly at night, the larva resting low in the grass during the day. The larval stage lasts eight to nine months.

Pupa

The pupa is green with black stripes on the wing cases, and is suspended from a pad of silk attached to a grass stem or other support, the larval skin being retained. The pupal stage lasts from three to four weeks.

♂ upper side; wingspan 40 mm.

♀ upper side; wingspan 47 mm.

BUTTERFLY
EGG
LARVA
PUPA

Distribution
England, particularly in the south, Wales, and southern Ireland.

Habitat
Grassy places, woodland rides, and along hedgerows, hence its two English names.

Life cycle
One generation a year. Over-winters as a young larva.

Larval foodplants
Grasses, such as annual meadow (*Poa annua*), cock's foot (*Dactylis glomerata*), and couch (*Agropyron repens*).

Butterfly
The ground colour is brownish-orange with dark brown margins. Near the apex of the forewing is a black spot which usually contains two white dots, and there is a white-pupilled spot near the anal angle of the hindwing. The underside of the hindwing is marked with shades of brown and white-centred spots. Males are smaller and brighter than the females, and have a conspicuous dark band of scent scales in the central area of the forewing.

Variation occurs frequently in the number and size of the eye-spots.

The butterfly can be found on the wing during July, August, and early September. It is a frequent visitor to flowers, and likes to bask with its wings open.

Egg
When ovipositing, the female crawls down to the base of the grasses, and deposits a single egg, which is usually attached to a grass blade or stem, but sometimes is merely dropped. The colour of the egg when first laid is pale yellow, but after a few days it becomes paler and blotched with reddish-brown. There are sixteen longitudinal keels. The egg hatches after about three weeks.

Larva
The newly emerged larva is cream-coloured with reddish-brown stripes. After the first moult the head and body are green, this colouring being

Underside

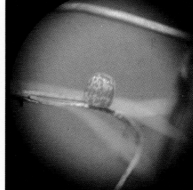

Egg; height 0·6 mm.

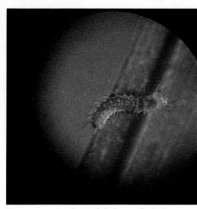

Larva, one day old; length 1·6 mm.

Fully grown larva; length 23 mm.

Pupa; length 12 mm.

retained after the second moult. In the final instar, after the fourth moult, the colour varies from ochreous to greenish-ochre, with dark lines. The anal points are ochreous, and the body is covered with short hairs.

The larva consumes part of the eggshell on emergence, then feeds on grasses until October, when hibernation begins, low down among the grass stems, and lasts until the following March. The larva is rather sluglike, both in appearance and movements. It feeds only at night, resting low in the grass during the day. The larval stage lasts about nine months.

Pupa

This is pale ochreous, streaked and spotted with brown. It is suspended by tail hooks from the old larval skin which remains attached to a pad of silk spun on a grass stem, and it hatches after about three weeks.

SATYRIDAE **Small Heath**

♂ (*top*) and ♀ upper sides; wingspan ♂ 33 mm.,
♀ 37–40 mm.

Underside

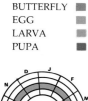

BUTTERFLY ■
EGG ■
LARVA ■
PUPA ■

Distribution
Throughout the British Isles.

Habitat
All types of grassy areas – fields,
hillsides, and downland.

Life cycle
Two generations a year. Over-
winters as a young larva.

Larval foodplants
Grasses, such as annual meadow
(*Poa annua*), woodland meadow
(*Poa nemoralis*), meadow fescue
(*Festuca pratensis*).

Butterfly
The upper side of the wings is tawny, with a black
sub-apical spot on the forewing. The male has
darkish borders which in the female are far less
noticeable. The underside of the hindwing is

greyish marked with white. Females are larger,
often considerably so.

Minor variation is common, particularly on the
underside.

The butterfly visits flowers such as thistles and
knapweeds, but it does not sit with its wings
open.

Egg
The eggs are laid singly on grass blades, usually
about 3 cm. above ground level. When first laid
they are green, but after a few days become ochreous with reddish-brown blotches. There are about
fifty fine longitudinal keels. The eggs hatch after
about a fortnight.

Larva
Directly after emergence, the larva is ochreous
with reddish-brown stripes, becoming green
when feeding commences. After the fourth, final
moult, the body is green with green and whitish-

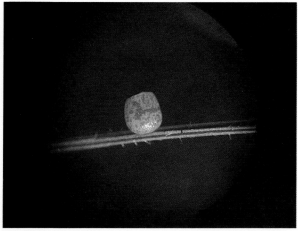

Egg; height 0·7 mm.

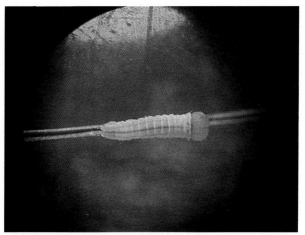

Newly hatched larva; length 1·6 mm.

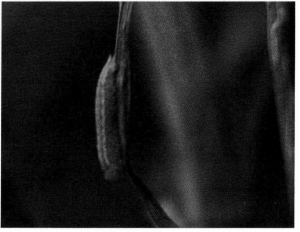

Fully grown larva; length 18 mm.

Pupa; length 8·5 mm.

green lines. The anal points are white and pink.

A partial hibernation begins when cold weather sets in – usually about the beginning of October. Movements are sluggish, and feeding takes place mainly at night. The larval stage lasts about five weeks, except in overwintering larvae, when it lasts about nine months.

Pupa

Suspended by tail hooks from a pad of silk spun on a grass stem, the pupa is green with dark brown markings on the wing cases. The larval skin is not retained, and the pupa hatches after three to four weeks.

SATYRIDAE **Large Heath**

Sspp. *scotica*, *above*, and *polydama*, upper sides; wingspan 41 mm.

Ssp. *scotica*, underside

BUTTERFLY
EGG
LARVA
PUPA

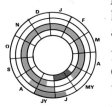

Distribution
Scotland, Ireland, northern England, north and mid-Wales.

Habitat
Boggy hillsides and marshes up to about 600 metres.

Life cycle
One generation a year. Overwinters as a young larva.

Larval foodplants
White beak-sedge (*Rhynchospora alba*). In captivity, and probably also in the wild, fescues.

Butterfly
There are three distinct subspecies, the geographical boundaries of which are rather ill-defined, and therefore two adjoining subspecies may overlap. They are:

(a) *davus* (also called *philoxenus*) – the southern race – found in Lancashire, Westmorland (Cumbria), Cheshire, and south Yorkshire. The upper side is dark brown in the male, rather paler in the female, with well-marked eye-spots; undersides with large conspicuous white-pupilled eye-spots.

(b) *polydama* (also called *tiphon*) – the central race – found in north Wales, Ireland, Northumberland, Cumberland (Cumbria), and north Yorkshire. Upper side lighter than *davus*, with less well-marked spots. Underside brownish and grey, with white markings and ill-defined eye-spots.

(c) *scotica* (also called *laidion*) – the northern race – found in Scotland, the Outer Hebrides, Orkney and Shetland Islands, and the Isle of Arran. Upper side tawny, underside of hindwing greyish with white marks, much resembling the Small Heath.

Minor variations in colour are fairly common.

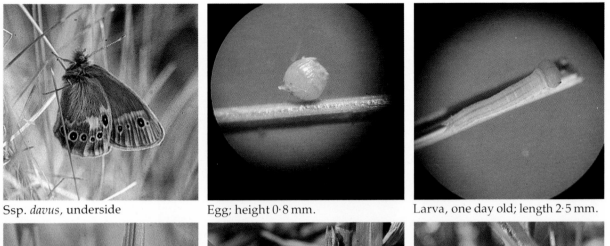

Ssp. *davus*, underside   Egg; height 0·8 mm.   Larva, one day old; length 2·5 mm.

Larva before second moult; length 6 mm.   Fully grown larva; length 25 mm.   Pupa; length 11 mm.

The Large Heath is a very restless butterfly, taking longish flights, and being very difficult to approach, particularly in the unpleasant terrain which it favours. Females appear grey when in flight. Like the Small Heath, it does not rest with its wings open. Its favourite flowers seem to be heather, tormentil, and thyme.

Egg
Laid singly on the foodplant, it is at first greenish-white, but after a few days becomes brownish, with darker brown blotches. It has about fifty fine longitudinal keels, and hatches in about a fortnight.

Larva
When freshly emerged, the colour is ochreous with brownish lines, becoming green when it be-gins to feed. After the first moult it is green with whitish stripes. When fully grown after the fourth moult, the head and body are green, the body also having dark green and white stripes. The anal points are pink.

The larva begins hibernation after the second moult, usually during September, and recommences feeding during the following March. It feeds mainly at night, and the larval stage lasts about ten months.

Pupa
Green in colour with darker stripes on the wing cases, it is suspended by tail hooks from a pad of silk on a stem on or near the foodplant, and hatches after about three weeks.

SATYRIDAE **Ringlet**

♂ upper side; wingspan 48 mm.

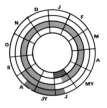

BUTTERFLY
EGG
LARVA
PUPA

Distribution
Most of England and Wales, in Scotland as far north as Aberdeen, and in Ireland.

Habitat
Clearings and rides in woods, and along hedgerows.

Life cycle
One generation a year, overwintering as a young larva.

Larval foodplants
Grasses, chiefly cock's foot (*Dactylis glomerata*), annual meadow (*Poa annua*), wood false brome (*Brachypodium sylvaticum*).

Butterfly
The ground colour is very dark brown, appearing almost black in the males – females are larger and paler, with more prominent eye-spots near the wing margins. The white-pupilled eye-spots on the undersides of both sexes are very conspicuous.

Variation occurs frequently in the number, size, and development of these eye-spots, ranging from ab. *lanceolata* (large oval-shaped eye-spots) to ab. *obsoleta* (complete absence of spots).

The Ringlet is a restless butterfly, which takes frequent short flights, showing a distinct preference for shade. Bramble flowers are its main source of food.

Egg
This is dome-shaped with a concave base, and is buff-white in colour. Like those of the Marbled White, the eggs are scattered freely amongst the grass, and they hatch after two to three weeks.

Larva
Directly after emergence, the ground colour is pale cream with darker lines. After the fourth and

♂ underside

Egg; height 0·7 mm.

Newly hatched larva; length 1·8 mm.

Fully grown larva; length 21 mm.

♀ underside

Larva in September; length 6 mm.

Pupa; length 11 mm.

last moult, the colour is ochreous with dark lines, a whitish lateral stripe, and ochreous anal points. The whole surface is covered with fine hairs.

The larva feeds until about October, when it enters into a partial hibernation, feeding during mild weather. It becomes fully grown in June, feeding only at night, and remaining low down among the grass stems during the day. The larval stage lasts about ten months.

Pupa
The ground colour is pinkish-ochre, speckled and streaked with brown. The pupa is formed on the ground at the base of the grass, and is completely unattached, being contained in a very slight cocoon formed of a few strands of silk. It hatches in about a fortnight.

♂ upper side; wingspan 44 mm.

♀ upper side; wingspan 47 mm.

BUTTERFLY

EGG

LARVA

PUPA

Distribution
England and Wales, commoner in the south. Local in Scotland. In Ireland only on the limestone of Co. Clare.

Habitat
Clearings in woods.

Life cycle
One generation a year, rarely two, the second producing butterflies in August. Overwinters as a young larva.

Larval foodplants
Dog violet (*Viola canina*). Also reported on primrose (*Primula vulgaris*).

Butterfly
The upper side is orange-brown marked with black. On the underside of the hindwing are two silver patches and a marginal row of silver lunules. The antennae are black with orange tips. Females are slightly larger and more yellow than the males, the pale marginal markings on the upper side of the hindwing are more prominent, and the wings are more rounded.

Variation often occurs in the amount of black marking on the upper side.

The flight is swift and gliding, and the butterfly eagerly visits bugle flowers.

Egg
Eggs are laid singly, usually on a stem or leaf of the foodplant, or on any other nearby plant. The eggs are whitish in colour, with twenty to twenty-five longitudinal keels, and hatch after about a fortnight.

Larva
When newly hatched, the body is ochreous with darker transverse bands, and covered with fine hairs. The head is shining black. After the first moult, the hairs are black and spiny, and after the second the ground colour becomes almost black. When fully grown after the fourth moult, the body is black and covered with conical spines which are all black except for two dorsal rows with yellowish bases.

Underside

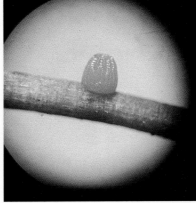

Egg; height 0·8 mm.

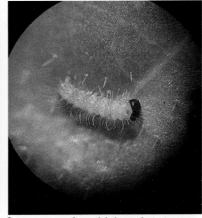

Larva, one day old; length 1·4 mm.

Larva, after second moult; length 8 mm.

Fully grown larva; length 24 mm.

Pupa; length 14 mm.

The larvae feed by day, and enter into hibernation at the beginning of August, after the third moult, usually inside dead curled-up leaves under or near the violet plants. Feeding begins again the following March, and takes place during the day, the larvae leaving the plant at night. The larval stage normally lasts ten to eleven months, but if a second generation is produced, the duration is only six to eight weeks.

Pupa
Hangs from a pad of silk spun on a stem, on or near the foodplant, and is brown in colour, much resembling a dead leaf. The stage lasts about ten days.

NYMPHALIDAE **Small Pearl-bordered Fritillary**

♂ upper side; wingspan 41 mm.　　　　♀ upper side; wingspan 44 mm.

Distribution
England, Wales, and Scotland.

Habitat
Open areas in woodlands, on moorland, grassy mountainsides, and some sea cliffs. It particularly favours damp areas.

Life cycle
One generation a year, rarely two, producing butterflies during August. Overwinters as a young larva.

Larval foodplant
Dog violet (*Viola canina*).

Butterfly
The upper side is orange-brown marked with black, and is very similar to that of the Pearl-bordered Fritillary, but may be distinguished by the darker colour on the upper side, and the presence of several more patches of silver on the underside of the hindwing. The antennae have orange tips. Females are larger and paler than males, and have more pronounced pale spots on the margins of the upper side.

Variation usually consists of an increase in the amount of the black marking.

The butterfly is a frequent visitor to flowers, especially bugle and heather, and often flies in company with the Pearl-bordered Fritillary, *B. euphrosyne*.

Egg
Eggs are laid singly, usually on a stem or the underside of a leaf of the violet plant, but sometimes are carelessly dropped. When first laid they are greenish in colour, this gradually fading to greyish. There are from eighteen to twenty longitudinal keels. Hatching takes place after about ten days.

Larva
Immediately after hatching, the head is shining black, and the body ochreous and covered with fine hairs. After the first moult, the ground colour is olive green with black spines. On emerging from hibernation, the body is ochreous with short black spines, and when fully grown after the fourth moult, the ground colour is dark brown with ochreous spines, of which the pair behind the head are long and directed forward over the head, which is black.

Underside

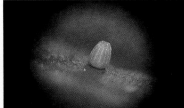

Egg; height 0·6 mm.

Larva, one day old; length 1·4 mm.

Larva after second moult; length 6 mm.

Larva after third moult; length 9·5 mm.

Fully grown larva; length 23 mm.

Pupa; length 14·5 mm.

The eggshell is eaten after emergence. The larva hibernates after the third moult, from the end of August until March, usually inside a dead, curled leaf. It feeds mainly by day, and is particularly active in sunshine, but rests away from the plant when not feeding. The duration of the larval stage is normally ten to eleven months, but if a second generation is produced, it is only six to eight weeks.

Pupa

The pupa is suspended by tail hooks from a pad of silk attached to a leaf or stem, either of the food-plant or a nearby plant, and is brown with darker markings. It hatches in about two weeks.

♂ upper side; wingspan 63 mm.

♀ upper side; wingspan 69 mm.

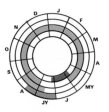

BUTTERFLY
EGG
LARVA
PUPA

Distribution
Most of England, Wales, and Scotland. Coastal districts of Ireland.

Habitat
Exposed grassy slopes, particularly near the coast, on moorlands, and sometimes in open woods.

Life cycle
One generation a year. Overwinters as a newly hatched larva.

Larval foodplant
Dog violet (*Viola canina*).

Butterfly
The upper side of the wings is rich orange-brown, marked with black. On the underside, the basal area of the hindwing is green with large silver spots; there is a marginal row of silver spots on the hindwing, and towards the apex of the forewing. The antennae have orange tips. Females are larger, paler, and have more conspicuous pale spots on the upper-side margin of the wings. Females of the Scottish race, ssp. *scotica*, are much more heavily marked with black.

Variation occurs in the extent of the black markings.

The flight of the Dark Green Fritillary is very strong and fast, and it is difficult to approach except when feeding from flowers, of which its favourites seem to be tall thistles.

Egg
Eggs are deposited singly on leaves or stems of the foodplant, and when first laid are primrose yellow, but after several days they become banded with purplish brown. There are about twenty longitudinal keels. The eggs hatch in two to three weeks.

Larva
When newly hatched, the head is black, and the body ochreous and covered with fine hairs. After the first moult the body is grey with black spines. After the second and third moults, the sides are marked with amber blotches and white stripes respectively. When fully grown after the fifth moult, the head is black, the body black speckled with white, with a line of reddish-orange blotches down the side, and covered with black spines.

On emergence, the young larva eats the eggshell, and then goes at once into hibernation at the base of the plant, beginning to feed during March. It is very active in sunshine, and can move quickly for a larva. The larval stage lasts about ten months.

Underside

Ssp. *scotica*, ♀ upper side

Egg; height 1 mm.

Larva, one day old; length 2·2 mm.

Fully grown larva; length 38 mm.

Cocoon

Pupa; length 21 mm.

Pupa

The head, thorax, and wingcases are blackish, and the abdomen orange-brown. A tent-like structure is made by drawing leaves together with silk low down near the base of the foodplant or a nearby plant, and the pupa is suspended inside by tail hooks from a pad of silk. This stage lasts about a month.

♂ upper side; wingspan 60 mm.

♀ upper side; wingspan 67 mm.

BUTTERFLY
EGG
LARVA
PUPA

Distribution
England and Wales, as far north as Cumbria.

Habitat
Woodlands and their outskirts.

Life cycle
One generation a year. Over-winters as an egg.

Larval foodplants
Dog violet (*Viola canina*), sweet violet (*V. odorata*).

Butterfly
The upper side of the male is bright orange-brown, marked with black spots and lines, and with two lines of black androconial scales on each forewing. On the underside, the basal area of the hindwing has green shading, the remainder of the wing is marked with silver spots, and towards the margin is a row of silver-pupilled red spots. The antennae are tipped with orange. Females are larger than the males, are more yellowish in colour, lack the scent scales, and have more rounded wings. The High Brown Fritillary is extremely difficult to distinguish from its near relative, the Dark Green Fritillary, even when the two are sitting on the same flower; the surest means of identification are the silver-pupilled red spots, and less green on the underside of the hindwing of *cydippe*.

Variation occurs in the amount of black marking on the upper side.

This is now a very scarce butterfly, having disappeared from many of its former haunts. The flight is swift and strong, and it is a very sun-loving species. Favourite flowers are thistles and brambles.

Egg
Eggs are deposited singly, either on stems or leaves of the foodplant, or on nearby vegetation. They have about fourteen prominent longitudinal keels. When newly laid, the eggs are yellowish in colour – this soon changes to reddish-apricot. As the larva develops inside, the egg becomes greyish, owing to the larva being visible through the shell – it remains in this state throughout the winter, and hatches about mid-February.

Larva
When just hatched, the colour is ochreous, marked with red-brown, the body is covered with

Underside

Egg; height 0·8 mm.

Egg during winter

Larva, one day old; length 2·2 mm.

Larva after third moult; length 10 mm.

Fully grown larva (dark form); length 38 mm.

Fully grown larva (light form)

Pupa; length 21 mm.

hairs, and the head is black. After both the first and second moults, the body is chequered with black and white, with short spines. After the third and fourth moults the spines are brownish-yellow. Fully grown, after the fifth moult, there are two distinct colour forms of the larva:
(a) Dark form: dark brown ground colour with a white dorsal stripe and pink spines.
(b) Light form: reddish-brown ground colour with a white dorsal stripe and reddish-brown spines.

During the first instar, the larvae will often feed on the violet flowers, and on the young leaves. Their presence is betrayed by the appearance of tiny notches in the edges of the leaves. When not feeding, larvae leave the plant, or rest in dead leaves at the base, and they invariably leave the plant at night. They are very active in sunshine, and can move extremely fast. The larval stage lasts two to three months.

Pupa

Suspended by tail hooks from a pad of silk spun under a leaf, or on a stem, often away from the foodplant, and enclosed in a tent made by drawing a few leaves together with silk, the pupa is dark brown with two rows of metallic greenish-gold spots. It hatches after three to four weeks.

♂ upper side; wingspan 72 mm.

♀ upper side; wingspan 76 mm.

BUTTERFLY ▪
EGG ▪
LARVA ▪
PUPA ▪

Distribution
Southern and midland counties of England, and Wales. Rare in northern England. Widespread in Ireland.

Habitat
Woodlands and their edges, and rough ground nearby.

Life cycle
One generation a year. Over-winters as a newly hatched larva.

Larval foodplants
Dog violet (*Viola canina*). In captivity, other species of violets.

Butterfly
On the upper side, the wings of the male are bright orange-brown, marked with black. Three of the veins on the forewing bear conspicuous patches of scent scales. The underside of the hindwings is iridescent green with four silver bands. The antennae are tipped with orange. Females are slightly larger, and are dimorphic – that is, there are two distinct forms. The more numerous of the two forms has a paler ground colour than the male, and with a somewhat greenish cast. The second, much scarcer form, known as *valezina*, has on the upper side the ground colour greenish-grey. On the underside the hindwing is similar to that of the normal form, but the ground colour of the forewing is pinkish-grey.

Variation occurs in the amount of the black marking, and, in the form *valezina*, in the shade of green and the amount of white on the upper side. Gynandromorphs have been taken with one side male and the other side *valezina* female.

The Silver-washed Fritillary is a sun-loving species, has a fast, strong flight, and frequently visits bramble blossom and thistles.

Egg
Eggs are laid singly in the crevices of the bark of trees which have dog violets growing in their vicinity. Trees most frequently chosen are oak, ash, and birch, and the egg is laid on the main trunk, up to a height of nearly two metres above the ground. The egg is whitish-green with twenty-five longitudinal keels, and it hatches in about a fortnight.

Pair: ♀ *above*, ♂ *below*

♀ *valezina:* underside

Fully grown larva; length 38 mm.

Underside

Egg; height 1 mm.

Larva hibernating; length 2·2 mm.

♀ *valezina:* upper side

Larva after second moult; length 10 mm.

Pupa; length 22 mm.

Larva

Directly after emergence, the head is black, and the body pale brownish-yellow with brownish blotches and fine hairs. After the first moult these hairs become black spines. After the third moult the ground colour is black with yellowish marks and lines. Fully grown after the fourth moult, the head is black, the body is dark brown and ochreous, with two prominent yellow dorsal stripes. The spines are reddish-ochre with black tips, and the first two behind the head are elongated, and project forward over the head.

When it emerges from the egg, the larva consumes its eggshell, and immediately spins a mat of silk in a crevice of the bark, on which it hibernates from August until the following March, when it goes in search of violet plants. It is very active, particularly in sunshine, and feeds during the day. The larval stage lasts about ten months.

Pupa

The pupa is suspended by tail hooks from a pad of silk either on the foodplant, or on some other nearby support. It is brownish in colour, with metallic gold patches, and hatches after about two and a half weeks.

♀ upper side; wingspan 48 mm.

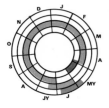

BUTTERFLY
EGG
LARVA
PUPA

Distribution
Central and western England, and Scotland to the Great Glen, Wales, Ireland.

Habitat
As its name suggests, it frequents marshy ground, but may also sometimes be found in drier areas, such as on hills where its foodplant occurs.

Life cycle
One generation a year. Over-winters as a third instar larva.

Larval foodplant
Devil's bit scabious (*Succisa pratensis*). Also reported on other scabious and plantains. In captivity, honeysuckle.

Butterfly
The upper side of the wings is reddish-brown with yellowish bands and black markings. The underside is similar, but less strongly marked.

The antennae have orange tips. Females are larger, with more rounded wings than the males. There are several distinct geographical races – the above description applies to ssp. *anglicana*, found in England and Wales. The race in Scotland – ssp. *scotica* – is much blacker in general appearance, while in Ireland – ssp. *hibernica* – the red and black are much more intense.

Variations in colour and pattern are quite frequent.

The Marsh Fritillary has recently disappeared from several of its former haunts, and is not nearly so common as it used to be. Colonies are quite close-knit, and the males are very active. Females fly less, and sit about with their wings spread in the sunshine. Flowers are eagerly visited.

Egg
Eggs are deposited in batches on the underside of a leaf of the foodplant. The basal area of each egg is smooth, but there are a number of ribs towards the crown. When first laid, the colour is yellow, changing after a few days to brown. Hatching occurs after about three weeks.

Eggs; height 0·8 mm.

Egg batch on underside of leaf

♂ underside; wingspan 42 mm.

Larvae, one day old; length 1·2 mm.

Hibernaculum

Larvae emerging from hibernation; length 7 mm.

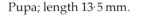

Fully grown larva; length 27 mm.

Pupa; length 13·5 mm.

Larva

The newly hatched larva is pale yellowish-brown, covered with fine hairs, and with a black head. After the first moult the colour is much darker, and spines replace the hairs. After the third moult, which takes place during hibernation, and until fully grown after the fifth moult, the head and spines are black, the body black with white speckles.

Soon after emergence, the larvae spin a dense web over the foodplant, beneath which they live and feed, moving to another plant when the first is consumed. During August a much more substantial web is constructed, inside which the larvae hibernate, emerging during February or early March to bask on sunny days; feeding recommences about a week later. During the final instar they dispense with the web and disperse, and can then be found singly. They suffer greatly from attacks by parasitic wasps such as *Apanteles* spp. The larval stage lasts about ten months.

Pupa

Buff-coloured, and marked with black and orange, the pupa is suspended by tail hooks from a silken pad attached to a stem or leaf near its foodplant, and hatches after about a fortnight.

♂ upper side; wingspan 41 mm.

♀ upper side; wingspan 47 mm.

BUTTERFLY ■
EGG ■
LARVA ■
PUPA ■

Distribution
The southern coast of the Isle of Wight.

Habitat
Rough grassy areas of undercliff.

Life cycle
One generation a year. Over-winters as a young larva.

Larval foodplants
Sea plantain (*Plantago maritima*), ribwort plantain (*P. lanceolata*).

Butterfly
The upper side of the wings is orange-brown marked with black. The underside of the hind-wing is straw-coloured with orange bands and black dots. The tips of the antennae are orange. Females are slightly larger than the males, and have more rounded wings and fatter bodies.

Variation occurs frequently in the amount of black on the upper side.

This butterfly was named after a Mrs Eleanor Glanville, who lived during the eighteenth century, and who was very interested in butter-flies. When she died, her will was contested on the grounds that this interest proved that she was of unsound mind. The range of the Glanville Fritillary in this country is extremely restricted – it occurs only on the southern coast of the Isle of Wight; colonies tend to remain in the same area year after year. The butterfly's flight is smooth and unhurried, and it frequently visits flowers.

Egg
The eggs are laid in large batches on the underside of a leaf of the foodplant. They are pale yellow in colour, and each has about twenty longitudinal keels running from the top to roughly half way down the side. Hatching occurs after about three weeks.

Larva
When just emerged, the head is black, and the body yellowish-white with fine hairs. After the second moult both the head and body are black, and following the third, the head is brown. When fully grown after the sixth moult, the head is red, the spines black, and the body black with white dots.

The habits of the larvae are similar to those of the Marsh Fritillary – they live gregariously under a web spun over the foodplant, and hibernate there after the fourth moult, from August until February, when they emerge to sun themselves,

Underside

Eggs; height 0·5 mm.

Eggs on plantain leaf

Larvae, one day old; length 1·25 mm.

Larval nest

Larvae in February; length 9 mm.

Fully grown larvae; length 25 mm.

Pupa; length 13·5 mm.

beginning to feed a few days later. After hibernation they remain in groups but dispense with the web. They are very active in sunshine, but huddle together deep in the grass when the weather is cool and dull. The larval stage lasts about ten months.

Pupa
Suspended by tail hooks from a pad of silk attached to a convenient stem, it is greyish in colour, marked with black and orange. The stage lasts about three weeks.

Heath Fritillary

♂ upper side; wingspan ♂ 40 mm., ♀ 44 mm.

BUTTERFLY ■
EGG ■
LARVA ■
PUPA ■

Distribution
Essex, Kent, Devon, and Cornwall.

Habitat
Clearings in woods.

Life cycle
One generation a year. Over-winters as a third instar larva.

Larval foodplants
Cow-wheat (*Melampyrum pratense*), plantain (*Plantago*), also foxglove (*Digitalis purpurea*), and wood sage (*Teucrium scorodonia*).

Butterfly
On the upper side, the wings are orange-brown marked with black. The underside of the hind-wing is whitish-yellow with orange bands and black marks, and the tips of the antennae are orange. Females are slightly larger, paler, less heavily marked, and have more rounded wings than the males.

Variation occurs quite frequently, mainly in the amount of black present on the wings.

The Heath Fritillary is diminishing in numbers and is now restricted to a few colonies in south-east England and in the West Country. Colonies tend to move their location in search of suitable habitats, i.e., clearings in woods where the under-growth has been cut down recently, thus allowing the cow-wheat to flourish. The butterfly has a slow, gliding flight, likes to bask in the sun, and eagerly visits flowers such as thistles and bugles.

Egg
Eggs are laid in large batches on the underside of a leaf of the foodplant. They are yellowish-white in colour, and each has about twenty-five longitudinal keels. They hatch in about a fortnight.

Larva
Immediately after emergence, the head is black, and the body ochreous-white and covered with fine hairs. After the second moult the body

Eggs; height 0·5 mm.

Eggs on plantain leaf

Underside

Larva emerging from egg

Larvae hibernating; length 3·5 mm.

Fully grown larva; length 24 mm.

Pupa; length 12·5 mm.

becomes brown, mottled with white, and with dark spines. After the sixth moult, fully grown, the head and body are black, and the dorsal spines amber-coloured.

After leaving the eggshells, the young larvae spin a web under a leaf of the foodplant, and live under it, feeding on the cuticle of the leaf. They hibernate from the end of August to the following March among dead curled-up leaves. After hibernation, they are only active in sunshine, and at other times rest low down among the leaves, or amongst dead leaves, and are difficult to find. Pheasants are particularly fond of them. The larval stage lasts about ten months.

Pupa
The pupa is suspended by tail hooks from a pad of silk attached to a convenient stem or leaf. It is whitish in colour, marked with orange and black, and the stage lasts about a fortnight.

NYMPHALIDAE **Red Admiral**

Upperside; wingspan ♂ 67 mm., ♀ 72 mm.   Underside

BUTTERFLY
EGG
LARVA
PUPA

Distribution
A migrant, it reaches all parts of the British Isles.

Habitat
Almost any type is suitable – gardens, hedgerows, rough ground, open woodland.

Life cycle
One or two generations a year. Some may overwinter successfully as butterflies.

Larval foodplants
Stinging nettle (*Urtica dioica*), pellitory of the wall (*Parietaria judaica*), hop (*Humulus lupulus*).

Butterfly
On the upper surface the ground colour is black. The forewing has a scarlet band, white blotches near the apex, and a trace of blue on the margin. In some individuals, a white dot may be present in the scarlet band. The hindwing has a band of scarlet along the margin, containing black dots, and there are blue markings at the anal angle. On the underside, the forewings are similar to the upper surface but with rather more blue. The hindwings are beautifully mottled with brown, bronze-green, and black. On the costal margin is a large cream-coloured blotch which tends to be more yellow in the female. Sexes are otherwise similar, although females are slightly larger. The antennae have ochreous tips.

Variation is rare – differences in the colour of the scarlet bands sometimes occur, or the forewing band may be broken up.

The Red Admiral is a migrant species which travels every year from southern Europe, reaching this country in spring, when it can be found in almost any type of habitat. In the autumn it is seen most frequently in gardens, where its favourite flowers are buddleia, Michaelmas daisy, and sedum. It is particularly fond of over-ripe fruit and exuding tree sap. A few individuals may hibernate, and there is some evidence of a return migration southwards in the autumn.

Egg
Very small, the egg is green in colour, with ten prominent glassy keèls. Just before hatching the colour becomes blackish. Eggs are laid singly on the upper surface of the young leaves of the foodplant, and hatch after about a week.

Vanessa atalanta (LINNAEUS)

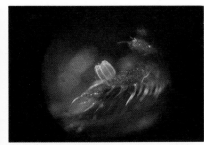

Egg; height 0·8 mm.

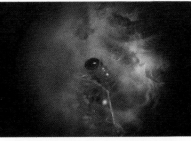

Larva, one day old; length 1·6 mm.

Larval tent

Larva before fourth moult; length 15 mm.

Fully grown larva (green form); length 35 mm.

Fully grown larva (brown form)

Pupa; length 23 mm.

Larva

Immediately after hatching, the body is rather hairy and greenish-ochre in colour; the head is black. After the first and second moults the body is olive brown, spiny, and has a rather greyish appearance. In the later instars there are several colour forms of the larva, and when fully grown after the fourth moult, the colour may be black speckled with white, with yellow spines and yellow marks along the sides, or grey-green marked with yellow-green, or brown with black spines, or with yellowish spines.

On emergence, the eggshell is not eaten, the larva going immediately to the base of the young leaf, where it constructs a tent by pulling the edges of the leaf together with silk. As it grows, the larva constructs larger homes, which become quite conspicuous. When nearly fully grown, the larva frequently cuts through the stem and pulls over the whole of the shoot to make a home in which it rests, usually in the shape of a J. It is solitary all its life, and suffers greatly from attacks by parasites. The larval stage lasts about a month.

Pupa

This is greyish, marked with gold, and is suspended by tail hooks from a pad of silk inside its last larval tent. It hatches after about two and a half weeks.

♂ upper side; wingspan 65 mm.

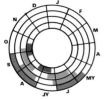

BUTTERFLY ■
EGG ■
LARVA ■
PUPA ■

Distribution

Uncertain, as this species is a migrant from North Africa. It has been recorded throughout the British Isles.

Habitat

Rough ground, hillsides, and lanes.

Life cycle

One to two generations a year. It cannot survive our winter in any stage, being killed off by the arrival of the cold weather at whatever stage has been reached.

Larval foodplants

Thistles (*Carduus* spp.). Also reported on burdocks (*Arctium*), mallows (*Malva*), and stinging nettle (*Urtica dioica*).

Butterfly

On the upper side, the ground colour is usually tawny-orange, though on fresh specimens there may be a distinctly pink flush. The wings are marked with black. The forewing has several white marks towards the apex, and the hindwing bears two blue markings at the anal angle. On the underside, the forewing is similar to the upper side, while the hindwing is beautifully patterned with ochre, white, olive green, and blue. The tips of the antennae and the legs are whitish. The sexes are similar, females being slightly larger and having more rounded wings.

Variation is very uncommon, but does sometimes occur in the extent of the black markings.

The Painted Lady is a frequent visitor to gardens. Its source of food is the nectar of flowers. Its flight is swift and strong, and each butterfly has its own territory which it patrols constantly, returning again and again to settle on the same spot. It is

Underside

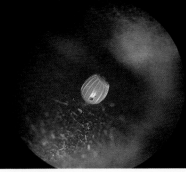

Egg; height 0·6 mm.

Larva, one day old; length 1·5 mm

Larval home

Fully grown larva; length 28 mm.

Pupa; length 24 mm.

active in sunshine, and is also crepuscular, often remaining active until well after dusk. Unlike most other species, pairing usually takes place during the late afternoon.

Egg
This is very small, green in colour, and has sixteen prominent longitudinal keels which give the egg a very glassy appearance. Eggs are laid singly on a leaf of the foodplant, usually on the upper surface, and hatch after about a week.

Larva
When newly emerged, the head is shining black, and the body greenish-ochre with fine black hairs. The ground colour is darker during the second instar, and after the second moult it becomes black with yellow lines and darker spines. When fully grown after the fourth moult, the head and body are black, and the body bears yellow markings, the most prominent being a yellow stripe along the side. The spines may be black or yellowish.

The newly hatched larva does not eat its egg-shell, but goes at once to the underside of the leaf and spins a silken shelter in which it lives, feeding on the lower cuticle of the leaf. As it grows and consumes the leaf, it moves upwards to a higher leaf, under which it continues to spin a new tent, until the last instar, when it feeds in the open. While the larva is resident in its tent, frass collects in large quantities on the silk, making the abode rather messy and increasingly conspicuous. The larval stage lasts about a month.

Pupa
Attached by tail hooks to a pad of silk, the pupa is formed in a tent-like structure similar to the larval home, either on or near the foodplant. It is greyish in colour, marked with brown and metallic gold, and lasts about a fortnight.

NYMPHALIDAE **Small Tortoiseshell**

Upper side; wingspan ♂ 50 mm., ♀ 56 mm.

BUTTERFLY
EGG
LARVA
PUPA

Distribution
Throughout the British Isles.

Habitat
Almost any type of country.

Life cycle
Two generations a year. Over-winters as a butterfly.

Larval foodplant
Stinging nettle (*Urtica dioica*).

Butterfly
On the upper side, the ground colour is reddish-orange, with patches of black, white and yellow. The margins of both fore and hindwings bear blue lunules. The underside is mainly blackish-brown, marked with paler areas. The antennae are tipped with yellow. The sexes are similar, females being slightly larger.

Variation is fairly frequent, and usually consists of differences in the shade of the ground colour, and in the extent of the black markings.

The Small Tortoiseshell may be found in almost any type of habitat, and is a frequent visitor to gardens, where it feeds eagerly from flowers, especially buddleia, sedum, and Michaelmas daisy. It hibernates as a butterfly from about October onwards, usually in sheds or outhouses, and will often settle down in the house, where unfortunately the central heating frequently awakens it prematurely. Hibernating individuals normally appear during February or March. Pairing takes place in the spring, usually during the late afternoon, and side by side, with the male's abdomen curved round to join that of the female.

Egg
The eggs are laid in a batch on the underside of a young nettle leaf. Short, young nettles are chosen in preference to older, taller plants. If a female intending to lay eggs comes across another female in the act of ovipositing, she will often attempt to deposit her own eggs on the same leaf at the same

Eggs; height 0·8 mm.

Egg batch on underside of nettle leaf

Underside

Eggs hatching

Larva, one day old; length 1·25 mm.

Larvae before third moult; length 8·5 mm.

Fully grown larva (light form); length 22 mm.

Pupa; length 21 mm.

time, thus causing great congestion. Each egg has nine prominent longitudinal keels. When newly laid, the colour is clear green, but after a few days this changes to a more yellowish-green. Hatching takes place after about ten days.

Larva

When newly emerged the head of the larva is black, and the body greenish-ochre with fine black hairs. After the first moult the ground colour is pale primrose yellow, and this colouring becomes gradually darker during the next instars. After the fourth and final moult, fully grown, the colouring varies. It can be yellowish, densely speckled with black and marked with yellowish lines and spines, or it may be black with yellowish spines.

The eggshells are not eaten. Immediately after emergence, the larvae spin a web of silk over the terminal leaves of the nettle. When these leaves are consumed, they move to the head of an adjacent nettle and spin another web. They are gregarious until the last instar, when they dispense with a web, and live either in small groups of two or three, or singly. Single larvae sometimes spin the edges of a nettle leaf together to form a shelter similar to that produced by the young Red Admiral larva. The larval stage lasts about a month.

Pupa

Suspended by tail hooks from a pad of silk attached to a stem, not usually on the foodplant unless in a large nettle-bed. The colour varies from darkish brown to a pinkish-brown with patches of gold. This stage lasts just under a fortnight.

Upper side; wingspan ♂ 64 mm., ♀ 70 mm.

Underside

BUTTERFLY ■
EGG ■
LARVA ■
PUPA ■

Distribution
Formerly reported from most counties of England and Wales – now extremely scarce.

Habitat
Large open woodlands, the verges of woods, or the vicinity of elms.

Life cycle
One generation a year. Over-winters as a butterfly.

Larval foodplants
Elm (*Ulmus*), sallow and willow (*Salix*), cherry (*Prunus*). Also reported on aspen and poplar (*Populus*), and whitebeam (*Sorbus*).

The Large Tortoiseshell may be distinguished from the Small Tortoiseshell by its larger size, paler orange colouring, the absence of white on the forewing, and the presence of seven black spots on the upper-side forewing, whereas the Small Tortoiseshell only has six.

The butterflies frequently bask in the sun with their wings open, and have a preference for tree sap, though they also visit flowers. They go into hibernation during August in hollow trees or outbuildings, and emerge during March. Pairing takes place in spring, side by side, as with the Small Tortoiseshell, and usually underneath some form of shelter. This species is now extremely rare, and this may be due largely to the attacks of parasites on the larvae.

Butterfly
The ground colour of the upper side is brownish-orange, marked with black and yellowish-ochre. The hindwing has a marginal row of blue lunules, and the antennae are tipped with yellow. The underside is mottled with shades of brown and purple, and the cell of the hindwing contains a whitish dot. The undersides of the wings are very bristly. The sexes are similar, females being slightly larger.

Variation is extremely rare.

Egg
Egg-laying takes place about two weeks after pairing. The eggs are deposited in neat batches encircling a twig, usually one of the topmost twigs of the elm, although the batch depicted in the photograph was found on an upper twig of a small sallow bush approximately 75 cm. above ground level. Each egg has about eight glassy longitudinal keels which give it a frosted appearance. When just laid, the colour is yellowish-orange, which gradually darkens to amber-brown, blending

Eggs; height 0·8 mm.

First instar larvae; length 5 mm.

Fully grown larvae; length 45 mm.

Egg batch   Eggs hatching   Second instar larvae; length 12 mm.   Pupa; length 25 mm.

beautifully with the bark on which the eggs are laid. They hatch after about three weeks.

Larva

Directly after emergence, the head is black and the ground colour pale ochre with fine black hairs. After the first moult, the ground colour becomes speckled with black, and with ochreous tubercles. After the fourth and last moult the head and body are black, the body is speckled with white and marked with orange lines; the spines are yellowish-orange, and are very sharp.

The larvae do not consume the eggshells, but directly after emergence go to the tip of the twig, spin a web under a leaf, and feed on the cuticle. As they grow, and consume the leaves, they move round the twigs, constructing fresh webs, which are very conspicuous. In the later stages, the larvae dispense with webs, but remain gregarious. The larval stage lasts about a month.

Pupa

Suspended by tail hooks from a pad of silk, either on the foodplant or some other support; the colour is pinkish-brown, marked with gold spots. The butterfly hatches after about a fortnight.

NYMPHALIDAE **Peacock**

Upper side; wingspan 63 mm.

BUTTERFLY
EGG
LARVA
PUPA

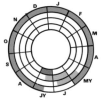

Distribution
Throughout the British Isles, with the exception of northern Scotland.

Habitat
Any type of country.

Life cycle
One generation a year. Overwinters as a butterfly.

Larval foodplant
Stinging nettle (*Urtica dioica*).

Butterfly
On the upper side, the ground colour is brownish-red, with distinctive blue and black 'peacock' eye markings. The underside of the wings is almost black, crossed by fine black lines, and with a whitish dot in the centre of the hindwing. The legs and the tips of the antennae are ochreous. The sexes are similar, although females are usually slightly larger.

Variations are not common, but very occasionally specimens are found in which the eye markings are completely blank – these are referred to as 'blind' Peacocks.

The butterfly feeds on the nectar of flowers, and can be found wherever these are present – hemp agrimony and buddleia are particular favourites. The Peacock hibernates as a butterfly, the majority from October until March, usually in sheds, hollow trees, wood piles, and houses. Some individuals, however warm the weather, will go into hibernation during August. Flying recommences in March, and pairing occurs soon afterwards. The butterfly can produce an audible rustling sound by opening and closing its wings.

Egg
The eggs have eight longitudinal keels, and are olive green in colour. They are laid in batches on

Underside

Newly hatched larva; length 1·6 mm.

Pupa (dark form)

Larvae before fourth moult; length 24 mm.

Eggs; height 0·8 mm.

Fully grown larvae; length 42 mm.

Pupa (light form); length 26 mm.

the undersides of young nettle leaves, and hatch in about a fortnight.

Larva

Directly after emergence, the head is black and the body ochreous green with fine black hairs. After the first moult the ground colour is olive brown, and this colour darkens through the following instars until the larva is fully grown after the fourth moult, when it is velvety black, with white dots and black spines. The prolegs are ochreous.

The eggshells are not eaten after emergence, the larvae going at once to the terminal leaves of the nettles, where they spin a dense web of silk. They live gregariously, moving from one nettle to another in groups, and both the occupied and deserted webs are very conspicuous. During the final instar they disperse over a wider area and dispense with the web. The larval stage lasts about a month.

Pupa

Suspended by tail hooks from a pad of silk attached to any suitable support; the colour varies from yellowish-green marked with pink and gold, to grey, or brownish-grey marked with black. The pupa hatches after about a fortnight.

NYMPHALIDAE **Comma**

♂ upper side; wingspan 55 mm.

♂ underside

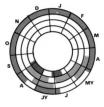

Distribution
Southern and midland counties of England, and in Wales.

Habitat
Clearings and rides in woods, on hillsides, and in gardens.

Life cycle
Two generations a year. Over-winters as a butterfly.

Larval foodplants
Hop (*Humulus lupulus*), stinging nettle (*Urtica dioica*), currant (*Ribes*), and has been reported on sallow (*Salix*) and elm (*Ulmus*).

Butterfly

The jagged outline of the wings is unique among British butterflies. The upper side is a rich orange-brown colour, marked with black and yellowish brown. The underside is marked in shades of brown and bronze-green, and in the centre of the hindwing is a white comma-shaped mark, from which the species gets its English name. The antennae are tipped with yellowish white, and the legs are whitish. Females are larger than the males, have slightly less ragged edges to their wings, and their undersides are darker. A proportion of the butterflies appearing in June and July are of the form known as *hutchinsoni*. In these individuals, the ground colour is paler and brighter on the upper side, and paler on the underside.

Variation may occur in the size and extent of the black markings, or in the shape of the comma mark. Underside colouring often varies from one individual to another.

The butterfly is commonly met with in the countryside, and it is a frequent visitor to gardens, where it is particularly fond of over-ripe fruit in the autumn. The flight is strong and swift, and on the wing the Comma may easily be mistaken for one of the larger Fritillaries. Butterflies from the second generation hibernate on tree trunks, in dense undergrowth, or in hedges, and the resemblance of the underside of the wings to a dead leaf forms an excellent camouflage. Pairing occurs in the spring.

Egg

Eggs are laid either singly or in groups of two or three, usually on the upper surface of a leaf of the foodplant, and often towards one edge. Each egg has about eleven longitudinal keels, which give it a very glassy appearance. The colour is green,

♀ underside

Eggs; height 0·75 mm.

Larva, one day old; length 2 mm.

Fully grown larva; length 34 mm.

F. ♀ *hutchinsoni:* underside

Second instar larva; length 4 mm.

Pupa; length 21 mm.

gradually becoming yellowish. Hatching takes place after about two and a half weeks.

Larva
Directly after emergence, the head is black, and the body greenish-ochre, with long black hairs. After the first moult the colour becomes brownish with white patches, and spines replace the hairs. Its resemblance to a bird dropping increases, until fully grown after the fourth moult, when the rear half of the body on the dorsal surface is pure white with white spines. The remainder of the body is black, heavily marked with orange-yellow, and with yellowish spines. The head is black and the crown strongly lobed.

The eggshell is not eaten on emergence, the larva going at once to the underside of the leaf, where it spins a web on which to rest, and soon perforates the surface of the leaf. It remains solitary all its life. When feeding on stinging nettle, and moving on to a new leaf, the larva will clear an area on which to rest by biting off the spines from the back of the leaf. The larval stage lasts six to seven weeks.

Pupa
Suspended by tail hooks from a pad of silk, either on the foodplant, or some nearby support. The colour is pinkish-brown marked with black, and with metallic gold or silver spots. It hatches after about two and a half weeks.

♂ upper side; wingspan 75 mm.

♀ upper side; wingspan 84 mm.

BUTTERFLY ■
EGG ■
LARVA ■
PUPA ■

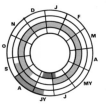

Distribution
Central southern England and the midlands.

Habitat
Large oak woods.

Life cycle
One generation a year. Over-winters as a third instar larva.

Larval foodplant
Broad leaved sallow (*Salix caprea*).

Butterfly
The upper side of the wings of the male are brownish-black, marked with white spots and lines, and shot with iridescent purple, which changes in extent according to the angle from which the wings are viewed. At the anal angle on each hindwing is a tawny mark, and a black spot with a tawny surround. The tips of the antennae are orange, the legs greyish-white, and the proboscis yellow. The female is larger than the male, has a browner ground colour, slightly larger white markings, and completely lacks the purple colouring. In both sexes, the white markings on the underside are similar to those above. The ground colour is shades of reddish-brown and pinkish-grey, with a large eye spot on the forewing.

Variation is extremely rare, but may consist of a reduction in the amount of white on the upper side. An extreme form with no white markings at all is known as ab. *iole*.

The Purple Emperor is a rare species which may escape notice, because it frequents the tops of tall oaks and ashes, and sometimes will not fly even though the weather seems suitable. Its flight is strong and fast, and it is a fearless insect, chasing other butterflies and even birds which venture too close to its resting place. Flowers do not seem to attract it, but it comes readily to various noxious substances such as cow-pats, carrion, and dirty puddles. It feeds from the honeydew left by aphids, and sucks up minerals from roads or tracks. Cars seem to fascinate it, and it will often attempt to get into a parked vehicle, or rest on the bonnet. The courtship flight begins round the top of a tree. The pair then spiral earthwards, ascend again to the treetops, and eventually the female settles on the topmost foliage, and the male walks round her, rapidly vibrating his wings, before pairing takes place.

Egg
The egg has fourteen longitudinal keels, and is green when first laid, but after about five days a purple zone develops near the base. Eggs are laid

Apatura iris (LINNAEUS)

First instar larva; length 3·5 mm.

Fully grown larva; length 42 mm.

Second instar larva; length 7 mm.

♀ underside

Egg; height 1 mm.

Larva hibernating; length 9 mm.

Pupa; length 30 mm.

singly on the upper surface of a leaf of the food-plant, usually towards the leaf edge, and hatch after about a fortnight.

Larva
When newly emerged, the head is black, and the body greenish-yellow. After the first moult the ground colour is green with yellow side stripes and a yellow 'saddle' mark. The last segment has two anal points which are ochreous, and the head bears a pair of ochreous horns. The whole body surface has a rather granular appearance. During hibernation the colour changes to one which matches the surface on which the larva is fixed, becoming green again after feeding recommences. When fully grown after the fourth moult, the general shape is slug-like, with a granular surface. The colour is green with yellow markings, and the horns on the head have reddish tips. When at rest,

these horns are kept resting flat on the leaf.

The eggshell is eaten on emergence. The young larva then spins a mat of silk on the midrib of the leaf, near the tip, on which it rests, leaving it only to feed. It begins hibernation during late October, after the second moult. The site chosen for hibernation is usually the fork of a twig, or a scar in the bark, or on a leaf which has been secured to the stem with silk. Feeding recommences during March. The larval stage lasts about ten months.

Pupa
Suspended by tail hooks from a pad of silk attached to the underside of a sallow leaf. The chosen leaf is secured to the stem by silk. The pupa is very leaf-like in appearance, being flattened in shape, pale green in colour, and marked with whitish lines which resemble the veins of the leaf. It hatches after about a fortnight.

NYMPHALIDAE **White Admiral**

♀ upper side; wingspan 64 mm.

♂ underside

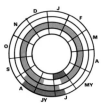

BUTTERFLY
EGG
LARVA
PUPA

Distribution
The south, south midlands, and the east of England.

Habitat
Large woods.

Life cycle
One generation a year. Over-winters as a third instar larva.

Larval foodplant
Honeysuckle (*Lonicera periclymenum*).

Butterfly

The upper side is brownish-black, marked with white. The underside is beautifully patterned in orange-red, white, black, and blue-grey. The antennae are tipped with orange and the legs are greyish. Females are slightly larger than males and have a lighter ground colour.

Variation is rare, but when it occurs it consists of a lessening of the extent of the white markings on the upper side.

The White Admiral was known in the early days of entomology as the 'White Admirable'. Its flight is gliding and leisurely, and it frequently visits flowers, in particular bramble and alder buckthorn. During dry weather it will settle on the ground to obtain minerals and moisture.

Egg
When ovipositing, the female usually chooses thin, straggly honeysuckle growing along the edge of a ride, or overhanging a ditch. She tests several leaves with her antennae, then sits on the selected leaf with her wings held flat, curves her abdomen across the leaf, and deposits a single egg towards the edge of the upper surface. The surface of the egg has a honeycomb pattern and is covered with spines. The ground colour is olive green, and hatching takes place after about a week.

Larva
When newly hatched, the ground colour is greenish-ochre with a granular appearance, and the head is black. After the first moult the colour becomes brownish, covered with pale spines, and with a white lateral stripe. The colouring becomes more greenish until, fully grown after the fourth moult, the body is green on the back and sides, marked with yellow, and purplish beneath the

Ladoga camilla (LINNAEUS)

Egg; height 1 mm.

Larva preparing hibernaculum

Fully grown larva; length 27 mm.

Newly hatched larva; length 2 mm.

Larva hibernating

First instar larva on midrib; length 3 mm.

Larva after hibernation; length 8 mm. Pupa; length 21 mm.

white lateral stripe. The head is brownish, and the spines vary from reddish-brown to ochreous in colour.

The newly hatched larva eats its eggshell, and then takes up its abode on the midrib of the leaf, near the apex. It eats away the leaf on either side of the midrib, and extends the midrib itself with silk, covering both the silk and its own body with frass. Towards the end of August, after the second moult, it prepares for hibernation by securing a leaf to the stem with silk, and drawing the basal edges of the leaf together with silk to form a tent in which it rests, hibernating completely, until the following March or April. Feeding then recommences, but now the larva rests on stems, not on leaves. The larval stage lasts about ten months.

Pupa
Suspended by tail hooks from a pad of silk attached to a stem or leaf of the foodplant; the colour is green, marked with purplish-brown, and adorned with metallic spots. The unusual shape of the pupa, together with its colouring, give it a remarkable resemblance to a partly shrivelled honeysuckle leaf. It hatches after about a fortnight.

NEMEOBIIDAE **Duke of Burgundy Fritillary**

♂ upper side; wingspan 29 mm.

♀ upper side; wingspan 32 mm.

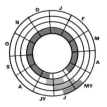

BUTTERFLY
EGG
LARVA
PUPA

Distribution
The southern half of England, and in Yorkshire and Lancashire.

Habitat
Clearings and rides in woods, sometimes hillsides.

Life cycle
One generation a year. Over-winters as a pupa.

Larval foodplants
Primrose (*Primula vulgaris*), cowslip (*Primula veris*).

Butterfly
The upper side of the wings is brownish-black, marked with tawny orange bands which are broken up into irregular spots. The spots near the outer margins have black dots in their centres. The fringes are white chequered with black. The underside of the forewing is similar to the upper side, but that of the hindwing is tawny orange marked with white patches, and with black dots near the margin. The antennae are black, ringed with white, and tipped with orange. Males have four walking legs, females have six. Females are also slightly larger, having rather more tawny orange on the upper side, and their wings are rounder in outline.

Variations are rare, but those which do occur take the form of an increase or decrease in the amount of black present.

The butterfly usually inhabits clearings and rides in woods, although it may sometimes be found on hillsides where the larval foodplants grow. It is very active, taking frequent short flights in between basking on low foliage.

Egg
The egg is globular and has no noticeable surface features. The colour is creamy-yellow until a day or two before hatching, when the young larva

Underside — Egg; width 0·6 mm. — Egg about to hatch

Larva, one day old; length 1·5 mm. — Fully grown larva; length 15 mm. — Pupa; length 11 mm.

inside becomes visible through the shell, and its long hairs give a latticed appearance to the egg. The eggs are deposited on the underside of a leaf of the foodplant, either singly or in groups of two or three, and hatch after about two weeks.

Larva

Just after emergence, the head is brownish-yellow and the body creamy-yellow, covered with long, dark, forked hairs. After the first moult the body is grey-green in colour, the hairs shorter and no longer forked. When fully grown after the third moult, the head and body are brownish. There is a purplish-brown dorsal line, and the body is densely covered with hair.

On emergence, the larva consumes the eggshell, and then commences feeding on the underside of the leaf, producing small perforations. During the first instar, when not feeding, it rests under the curved edge of the leaf, but during the subsequent instars it leaves the plant altogether, and rests among dead leaves beneath or near it. The larval stage lasts five to six weeks.

Pupa

Attached by tail hooks to a pad of silk, and by a silken girdle, to the underside of a leaf, often on the foodplant, the pupa is creamy-ochre, spotted and striped with black, and the whole surface is very bristly. This stage lasts throughout the winter.

LYCAENIDAE **Small Blue**

Upper side; wingspan 25 mm.

Pair: undersides

BUTTERFLY

EGG

LARVA

PUPA

Distribution
Small colonies in most parts of the British Isles where its larval food-plant occurs.

Habitat
Grassy slopes and downs.

Life cycle
One generation a year – in favour-able years two, producing butter-flies in August. Overwinters as a fully grown larva.

Larval foodplant
Kidney vetch (*Anthyllis vulneraria*).

Butterfly

The upper side of the male is sooty black with a dusting of silvery-blue scales. Females are slightly browner in colour, and lack the blue scales. The underside is pale grey, shading into pale blue at the base of the wings, and marked with white-ringed black dots. The antennae are black, ringed and tipped with white.

Variation sometimes occurs in the markings on the underside.

The haunts of the Small Blue are warm, sunny hollows on grassy slopes where the larval food-plant grows, such as chalk or limestone hills and downs. Colonies are often very small, and may cover only a few square metres. The flight is swift, and the butterfly frequently visits wild flowers.

Egg
The egg is greenish-white in appearance, with a dark area at the micropyle. The surface is covered with a fine raised network, giving it a lacy pattern. The eggs are very small, and are deposited singly on the calyces of the kidney vetch flowers, tucked in amongst the hairs, and usually hidden between adjoining calyces. They hatch in about a week.

Larva
Directly after emergence, the head is black and the body whitish-ochre, with long dark hairs. After the first moult the body colouring is yellow, marked with red, and the surface is more densely hairy. During the third instar, and fully grown in the fourth instar, the ground colour is pinkish-ochre with a dark line along the back, and dark marks along the sides. The surface is covered with

Egg; width 0·4 mm.

Hibernaculum

Larva after second moult; length 4 mm.

Fully grown larva; length 9·5 mm.

Pupa; length 8 mm.

short bristles, and the small head is shining black and borne on a retractile neck.

The eggshell is not eaten, and its presence is a good indication that a larva is resident in the flower head. On hatching, the larva bores through the calyx and feeds within on the developing seed. During the early instars the larvae are cannibals, and if two meet on the same flower head, one will devour the other. At about the end of July, when the larva is fully grown, it prepares for hibernation by spinning a silken shelter for itself either in a flower head, or low down amongst surrounding vegetation. The latter site seems more satisfactory, as the flower heads of the kidney vetch usually get blown to pieces by autumn winds. Hibernation lasts until the following May, when the larva pupates without feeding again. The larval stage lasts about eleven months except when a second generation is produced, when the duration is seven to eight weeks.

Pupa
Attached by tail hooks to a pad of silk, and by a silken girdle, to any suitable support. The one illustrated here was attached to a flower head of kidney vetch. The surface is distinctly hairy, the colour creamy buff marked with black; the head, thorax, and wing-cases are brownish-grey. The pupa hatches in about a fortnight.

LYCAENIDAE **Silver-studded Blue**

♂ upper side; wingspan 31 mm.

♀ upper side; wingspan 29 mm.

BUTTERFLY
EGG
LARVA
PUPA

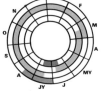

Distribution
England and Wales.

Habitat
Heathland, or on chalk and limestone.

Life cycle
One generation a year. Overwinters as an egg.

Larval foodplants
Gorse (*Ulex europaeus*), bird's foot trefoil (*Lotus corniculatus*), heather (*Erica*). Reported on other leguminous plants.

Butterfly
The upper side of the male is violet-blue with black borders and white fringes. On the underside the ground colour is bluish-grey marked with white-ringed black spots. The hindwing has a marginal orange band edged on the inside with black crescents, and on the outside by black spots centred with metallic blue, giving the butterfly its English name. The antennae are black, ringed and tipped with white, and the legs are white. Females are slightly smaller than the males, and the upper sides are brown with a wavy orange marginal band on the hindwings, usually extending on to the forewings. The undersides are similarly marked to those of the males, but the ground colour is light brown. The antennae are tipped with orange.

The descriptions above refer to the usual heathland subspecies, *argus*. Two other subspecies are found in the British Isles – *cretaceus*, larger and brighter, and occurring on chalk and limestone, and *caernensis*, smaller and earlier (mid June), whose larva is reported to feed on rock rose (*Helianthemum*), and which occurs on limestone in Caernarvonshire. The subspecies *masseyi* – males bright blue and females much more blue on the upper side – which formerly occurred on the Westmorland (Cumbria) and Lancashire mosses, has been extinct since a serious fire in its habitat in the early 1940s.

Variation occurs mainly in the spotting on the underside – some of the spots are occasionally confluent. The ground colour of the upper side may also vary, particularly in the male.

Pair, undersides: ♀ *left*, ♂ *right*

Egg; width 0·6 mm.

Larva, one day old; length 1·1 mm.

Larva after second moult; length 4 mm.

Fully grown larva; length 12·6 mm.

Pupa; length 8·5 mm.

The usual habitat of this species is heathland, but it also occurs on some chalk areas, coastal cliffs, and mosses. The butterflies are active, taking frequent short flights, and visiting flowers such as bramble and heather.

Egg

Eggs are laid singly on the underside of a leaf of the foodplant. They are white in colour, with a deep micropyle, and a delicate lacy pattern over the surface. They remain about eight months before hatching in the spring.

Larva

Just after emergence the head is black, and the body pale ochreous, bearing long hairs. After the first moult, brown and white longitudinal lines appear – this colouring remains unchanged until the third moult; in the final instars the head is black and the body green with a blackish-brown dorsal stripe bordered on each side by a white stripe. The sides are marked with oblique olive green dashes, and green and white stripes. Another colour form of the larva has a reddish-brown ground colour. The eleventh segment bears a pair of yellow-tipped retractile tubercles which it thrusts out when alarmed. It reaches full growth after the fourth moult.

The eggshell is not eaten. When feeding on gorse during the early instars, the larva eats the flowers, perforating the petals. When feeding on other legumes such as bird's foot, larvae eat the leaves. They feed by day and night, and this stage lasts about three months.

Pupa

Formed on the ground at the base of the foodplant or in its vicinity, the pupa is not attached, but lies on a pad of silk. The colour is ochreous with a brown streak down the abdomen and slightly greenish wingcases. It hatches after about two and a half weeks.

♂ upper side; wingspan 29 mm.

♀ upper side

BUTTERFLY
EGG
LARVA
PUPA

Distribution
England as far north as southern Yorkshire, and Wales.

Habitat
Rough grassy areas, particularly chalk and limestone downs and hillsides, and some sandy areas.

Life cycle
Two generations a year. Over-winters as a young larva.

Larval foodplants
Rock rose (*Helianthemum chamae-cistus* – also known as *H. rummu-larium*), common storksbill (*Erodium cicutarium*).

Butterfly
The wings of the male are dark brown on the upper side, with white fringes. On both wings there is a submarginal row of orange lunules – those on the forewing do not reach the apex. The forewing has a black discal spot. The underside of the wings is greyish-brown, marked with white-circled black spots; both wings have a submarginal band of orange spots. The antennae are black, ringed and tipped with white, and the legs are white.

The female has the upper side a slightly lighter brown, and the submarginal orange lunules on the forewing extend right to the apex. The underside is slightly browner, and the orange spots are slightly larger; otherwise the sexes are similar. No blue occurs on either sex, and this fact will help to distinguish the species from the browner females of the Common Blue.

Variation can occur in the ground colour of upper or underside, in the colour of the submarginal spots, and in the size and number of the black spots on the underside.

The Brown Argus is active in sunshine, and flies swiftly, often visiting flowers and basking on low vegetation. At night and in dull weather it rests on the flower stems of tall grasses.

Egg
Greenish-white in colour, with a conspicuous deep micropyle, the surface is covered with a raised network. Eggs are laid singly, usually on

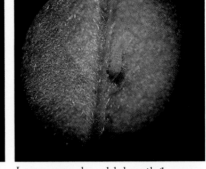

♂ underside   Egg; width 0·5 mm.   Larva, one day old; length 1 mm.

Larva, after third moult; length 7 mm.   Fully grown larva; length 11 mm.   Pupa; length 8 mm.

the underside of a leaf of the foodplant, where they are very difficult to see, and hatch after about a week.

Larva

When newly emerged, the head is black, the body pale yellow, bearing long hairs. The colour gradually becomes whitish-green, exactly matching the underside of a rock rose leaf. After the second and third moults the ground colour varies from green to yellowish-green, marked with reddish-pink. After the fourth and last moult, the head is black, the body green with short white hairs. There is a purplish-brown dorsal stripe, oblique dark green lines on the sides, and pink and purple stripes in the spiracular region. There is a pair of retractile tubercles on the eleventh segment similar to those of the Silver-studded Blue.

The eggshell is not eaten. The larva lives on the underside of a leaf, and in its early instars feeds on the lower cuticle, producing white and brown blotches on the leaf; during later instars the whole leaf is consumed. It is strongly associated with ants, particularly *Myrmica* spp. which 'milk' its honey gland; indeed, the presence of ants seems to be essential to its well-being. Larvae of the second generation hibernate after the second moult, either at the base of the plant or on the underside of a leaf, and recommence feeding during March or April. The larvae from the first generation are fully grown after about six weeks, while overwintering larvae become fully grown after about nine months.

Pupa

Brownish-green in colour, marked with rose-pink lines, and with a black 'eyebrow' mark. It is unattached, merely secured by a few threads of silk either between leaves, or more often at the base of the plant. It hatches after about a fortnight.

♂ upper side; wingspan 29 mm.

♀ upper side; wingspan 30 mm.

BUTTERFLY
EGG
LARVA
PUPA

Distribution
Scotland. In England as far south as Derbyshire.

Habitat
Rough grassy banks and hillsides where its larval foodplant grows.

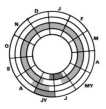

Life cycle
One generation a year. Over-winters as a young larva.

Larval foodplants
Rock rose (*Helianthemum chamaecistus*). Also reported on storksbill (*Erodium cicutarium*).

Butterfly
The upper side of the wings of the male is deep chocolate brown with white fringes. The hind-wing has a submarginal row of small orange lunules, a few of which are also found on the forewing. The discal spot on the forewing is white. The underside is brownish-grey marked with white spots which may sometimes be centred with tiny black dots. Both wings have a submarginal row of orange spots. The antennae are black, ringed and tipped with white, and the legs are white. Females are slightly larger than males, their upper side is a lighter brown, and the orange lunules are larger, extending almost to the apex of the forewing.

The southern race of *artaxerxes* is known as *salmacis*; this occurs from Derbyshire to the Scottish border. The discal spot is black, surrounded by white, and the white spots on the underside are centred with black dots. Until quite recently, both *artaxerxes* and *salmacis* were considered to be sub-species of *agestis*, but in 1967 Jarvis and Hoegh-Guldberg proved conclusively that *artaxerxes* was a separate species, and that *salmacis* was a sub-species of *artaxerxes*.

Variation can occur in the colour and size of the submarginal spots, and in the size and number of the spots on the underside.

The Northern Brown Argus is very active in sunshine, flies swiftly, and is difficult to approach. Colonies tend to be rather small and scattered. It is territorial in habit, the males especially having their own territories, which they patrol regularly. These territories are often at some distance from the larval foodplant. The butterfly visits flowers such as bird's foot trefoil and thyme.

♂ underside

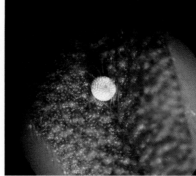

Egg; width 0·8 mm.

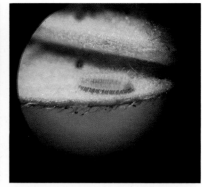

First instar larva; length 1·2 mm.

Larva hibernating after second
moult; length 4 mm.

Fully grown larva; length 13 mm.

Pupa; length 8 mm.

Egg
White in colour, with a depressed micropyle and a raised network pattern, it resembles those of the Brown Argus and the Common Blue. Ovipositing usually occurs early in the morning or during the late afternoon; the eggs are deposited singly on the upper surface of a foodplant leaf, and are very conspicuous. They hatch after about a week.

Larva
Directly after emergence, the head is black, the body yellowish-white and bearing long hairs. After the first moult the ground colour is pale green with a white subspiracular stripe. After the second moult this stripe is joined by a pink one. After the third moult, and until fully grown after the fifth moult, the head is black, the body green with short white hairs. There are oblique dark green side stripes, a dark dorsal stripe, and pink and white lateral stripes.

The eggshell is not eaten, the larva going at once to the underside of the leaf, where it eats a groove in the cuticle in which it rests. It is associated with ants, and often leaves the foodplant when not feeding. It goes into hibernation towards the end of September, after the second moult, either low down among the stems, or under a leaf of the foodplant, and emerges to bask in the sun during March. The larval stage lasts ten to eleven months.

Pupa
Brownish-green in colour, with a greenish thorax and wingcases, pinkish-brown markings on the abdomen, and a black 'eyebrow' mark. It is unattached, being formed either among leaves, or at the base of the foodplant, often on the ground, covered by a few silk threads and lying on a silk mat. The larval skin is retained, and the pupa hatches after two and a half to three weeks.

LYCAENIDAE **Common Blue**

♂ upper side; wingspan 35 mm.

♀ upper side; wingspan 35 mm.

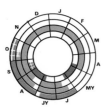

BUTTERFLY

EGG

LARVA

PUPA

Distribution
Throughout the British Isles.

Habitat
Rough ground, downland, and hillsides.

Life cycle
Two generations a year; in favourable years in the south, three. In the north, one generation a year. Overwinters as a young larva.

Larval foodplants
Bird's foot trefoil (*Lotus corniculatus*), lesser yellow trefoil (*Trifolium dubium*), restharrow (*Ononis repens*), prickly restharrow (*O. spinosa*), and clovers (*Trifolium*).

Butterfly
The upper side of the male is bright violet-blue with white fringes into which the black tips of the veins sometimes extend slightly. Both fore and hindwings are edged with a thin black line, and the veins are pale shining blue. On the underside the ground colour is greyish, marked with white-ringed black spots. Towards the wing margins is a row of orange lunules edged with black and white. The antennae and legs are black and white.

The female varies in the colouring of the upper side. It may be brown with a dusting of blue scales near the bases of the wings, or the blue shading may extend over the whole of the wings. The forewing has a row of orange lunules and black dots near the margin, and the hindwing has a row of black spots edged with orange and white. The markings on the underside are similar to those of the male, but the ground colour is brown.

Scottish and Irish specimens are larger, the males are brighter, and the females very blue.

Variation is common in this species, and consists of differences in the ground colour, and changes in the size and shape of the spots on the underside.

Numbers seem to have declined since this butterfly was given its English name, and it is not

♀ upper side (blue form)   Pair, undersides: ♂ *left*, ♀ *right*   Egg; width 0·6 mm.

Newly emerged larva; length 1 mm.   Fully grown larva; length 12·5 mm.   Pupa; length 9·5 mm.

found in nearly such profusion nowadays. It is active in sunshine, frequently visiting flowers, of which its favourites seem to be marjoram and fleabane. At night and in dull weather it rests head down on the flower stems of tall grasses.

Egg
Greenish-grey in colour with a raised white network and a sunken micropyle, the eggs are laid singly, usually on the upper surface of a leaf of the foodplant, although sometimes a female will deposit an egg on some other adjacent plant. Hatching takes place after about nine days.

Larva
When newly emerged, the head is brown and the body greenish-yellow, bearing long white hairs. During succeeding instars the ground colour becomes greener with yellowish sub-dorsal and lateral lines. When fully grown after the fourth moult, the head is black, the body bright green with darker green sub-dorsal and lateral lines, the surface bearing short white hairs. The tenth seg-

ment has a honey gland, and the eleventh segment a pair of retractile tubercles.

The eggshell is not eaten. The young larva goes either to the underside of the leaf, where it feeds on the cuticle, making white patches on the leaf, or into the flower head, where it feeds among the flowers. Larvae of the second generation go into hibernation after their second moult low down on the foodplant, on a mat of silk either under a leaf or on a stem, emerging during March. During the early instars they are very sensitive to vibration, and a footstep will cause them to drop off the plant. Larvae from the first generation are fully grown after about six weeks, while overwintering larvae are fully grown after about nine months.

Pupa
Greenish-ochre in colour, the pupa is formed either on the ground beneath the foodplant, or among the stems near the base. It is surrounded by a few threads of silk, and the larval skin is retained. This stage lasts about a fortnight.

LYCAENIDAE **Chalkhill Blue**

♂ upper side; wingspan 38 mm.

♀ upper side; wingspan 38 mm.

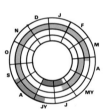

BUTTERFLY ■
EGG ▨
LARVA ▨
PUPA ■

Distribution
Southern and central England, on chalk and limestone.

Habitat
Chalk and limestone hillsides and downland.

Life cycle
One generation a year. Over-winters as an egg.

Larval foodplant
Horse-shoe vetch (*Hippocrepis comosa*). Also recorded on kidney vetch (*Anthyllis vulneraria*), and bird's foot trefoil (*Lotus corniculatus*).

Butterfly
The male is pale silvery blue on the upper side; the fringes are white chequered with black. The outer margin of the forewing is black; the hindwing has a marginal row of black spots edged with black and white. The underside is greyish, the hindwing being darker, and both wings are marked with white-ringed black spots. The hindwing has a submarginal row of black, white, and orange spots. The antennae are black and white with brown tips.

The female is brown on the upper side, with a white-ringed black discal spot on the forewing. The fringes are white, chequered with brown. The forewing has a row of pale orange submarginal marks, and the hindwing a submarginal row of black spots edged with white and orange. The markings on the underside are similar to those of the male, but the ground colour is brown.

Variation is very frequent in the Chalkhill Blue, and named aberrations are numerous. Three extreme forms are:

(i)   ab. *fowleri* – the border and the black spots on the outer margin are white instead of black.

(ii) ab. *syngrapha* – a variation of the female in which all of the wings out to the orange border is blue.

(iii) ab. *semisyngrapha* – another female variation in which the hindwing is as described above, and the forewing has the basal half blue.

The Chalkhill Blue is, as its English name suggests, confined to chalk and limestone hillsides and downland where its foodplant grows. It is an active butterfly, and can often be found in large numbers. It visits flowers, and often basks with its wings open on low vegetation. It can also be found feeding on animal droppings, particularly those of the fox.

♂ underside

♀ underside

Egg; width 0·5 mm.   Fully grown larva; length 16 mm.   Pupa; length 12 mm.

Egg

The egg is white in colour with a raised network pattern. The top is flat with a dark sunken micropyle. The female, when ovipositing, crawls right down into the herbage and deposits her eggs singly on any leaf or stem, not necessarily those of the foodplant. The egg remains there throughout the winter, hatching the following spring.

Larva

Directly after emergence the head is black and the body pale yellow, covered with long hairs. The ground colour becomes bluish-green, striped with yellow, after the second moult. When fully grown after the fourth moult, the head is black, the body green, with short brownish hairs. The sub-dorsal and lateral lines are rich yellow. The tenth and eleventh segments bear a honey gland and a pair of retractile tubercles respectively.

The eggshell is not eaten. The larva feeds on either leaves or flowers – when eating leaves, young larvae cause white blotches by eating the cuticle. When not feeding, they rest on the backs of the leaves, feeding mainly at night. The larval stage lasts about two and a half months.

Pupa

Ochreous in colour, the pupa is formed without any means of attachment, on the ground beneath the foodplant, concealed under the vegetation. It hatches after about a month.

LYCAENIDAE **Adonis Blue**

♂ upper side; wingspan 38 mm.

♀ upper side; wingspan 38 mm.

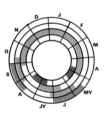

BUTTERFLY ■
EGG ■
LARVA ■
PUPA ■

Distribution
Southern England, chalk and limestone areas only.

Habitat
Chalk and limestone hills and downland.

Life cycle
Two generations a year. Overwinters as a young larva.

Larval foodplant
Horse-shoe vetch (*Hippocrepis comosa*).

Butterfly
The male is a brilliant sky-blue. The fringes are white with the vein ends showing in black. The outer margins of both wings are outlined with black. The underside of the forewing is dark grey, that of the hindwing brownish-grey – both are marked with white-ringed black spots. The outer margin of the hindwing has a row of black spots edged with white and orange. The antennae are black and white, tipped with orange.

The female is dark brown with a black discal spot on the forewing. The fringes are white, chequered with blackish-brown. The bases of the wings are dusted with blue scales, and the hindwing has a submarginal row of black spots edged with orange and blue. On the underside the markings are similar to those of the male, except that there is a row of submarginal orange spots on the forewing, and the ground colour is brownish.

Variation may occur in the size and extent of the black spots, and in the ground colour of the upper side in the male. The female variety ab. *ceronus*, in which the ground colour is blue, corresponds to ab. *syngrapha* in the Chalkhill Blue.

The Adonis Blue is very much scarcer and more localized than the Chalkhill Blue. The butterflies are active in sunshine, and have a swift flight, frequently visiting flowers.

Egg
Greenish-white in colour with a raised white network, a flattened top, and a depressed micropyle. Eggs are laid singly, usually on the underside of a leaf of the foodplant, but they may be attached to any part. They hatch in two to three weeks.

Larva
Immediately after emergence the head is black and the body pale yellow with hairs. In all instars

♂ underside

♀ underside

Egg; width 0·5 mm.

Newly hatched larva with eggshell; length 1 mm.

Larva after fourth moult; length 12 mm.

Fully grown larva; length 15·5 mm.

Pupa; length 11 mm.

the larva closely resembles that of the Chalkhill Blue, being green with yellow stripes, and when fully grown after the fourth moult, it is almost identical to that species, except that the ground colour is a darker green in the Adonis Blue, and the hairs are slightly darker.

The eggshell is not eaten. The young larva commences to feed on the lower cuticle of the horse-shoe vetch leaf, causing white blotches to appear. Larvae of the second generation hibernate on mats of silk either underneath a leaf, or low down among the stems, and begin feeding again towards the end of March. When not feeding they rest away from the plant. Larvae from the first generation are fully grown after about four to six weeks, while overwintering larvae are fully grown after about seven months.

Pupa

Ochreous in colour, the pupa is formed within a loose cocoon just below the surface of the soil, or under moss or debris on the surface. It is unattached, and hatches after about three weeks.

LYCAENIDAE **Large Blue**

♀ upper side; wingspan 43 mm.

BUTTERFLY
EGG
LARVA
PUPA

Distribution
Possibly extinct in the British Isles; until recently found in only one area of north Devon, but the species has now disappeared from all known localities.

Habitat
Grassy slopes with short turf and low scrub.

Life cycle
One generation a year. Overwinters as a young larva.

Larval foodplant
Wild thyme (*Thymus drucei*) in the early instars; later the larva feeds on the larvae of *Myrmica* ants.

Butterfly
The upper side of the male is blue with black borders and black spots. The underside is greyish, tinged with blue at the base of the wings, and marked with white-ringed black spots. The fringes are white, and the antennae black, ringed and tipped with white. Females are slightly larger than males, the wings are brighter and more heavily marked with black. The ground colour on the underside is slightly more brown.

Variation occurs chiefly in the number and size of the black spots on the upper side.

The habitats of the Large Blue are usually south-facing slopes with short turf and low scrub, where wild thyme grows and *Myrmica* ants are present. The flight is not particularly swift, and the butterfly visits flowers, including wild thyme.

Egg
The eggs are bluish-white with a raised network and a sunken micropyle. They are laid singly on thyme buds, and hatch in seven to ten days.

Larva
Directly after hatching the head is black and the body pale greenish-yellow, with long white hairs

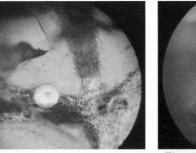

Egg; width 0·5 mm.

First instar larva; length 1 mm.

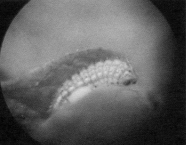

♀ underside

Second instar larva; length 2·5 mm.

Larva with ant

Larva in ants' nest (September); length 7 mm.

Pupa; length 12·5 mm.

After the first moult the ground colour becomes pink, and exactly matches the colour of the buds. When fully grown, the colour is pinkish-ochre.

The eggshell is not eaten. The young larva feeds on the thyme flowers, and in the first instar is cannibalistic, and will consume any other larvae it meets. After the second moult the larva drops from the plant and is found by an ant of the genus *Myrmica*, usually *M. sabuleti*, which proceeds to 'milk' the larva's honey gland. After a few hours, the ant picks up the larva and carries it into its nest. There it feeds on ant larvae until it is half grown, when it hibernates in the ant's nest. It recommences feeding in spring, the larval stage lasting about ten months.

Pupa

The pupa is brownish-ochre in colour, and is formed, without any attachment, inside the ants' nest. It hatches after about three weeks, and the butterfly crawls out of the nest before its wings expand.

LYCAENIDAE **Holly Blue**

♂ upper side; wingspan 35 mm.

♀ upper side; wingspan 35 mm.

BUTTERFLY
EGG
LARVA
PUPA

Distribution
England and Wales, commoner in the south. Local in Ireland.

Habitat
Woods, shrubby areas, hedgerows, and gardens.

Life cycle
Two generations a year. Overwinters as a pupa.

Larval foodplants
In spring, holly (*Ilex aquifolium*); in autumn, ivy (*Hedera helix*). Also reported on the flowers of dogwood (*Swida sanguinea*), berry-bearing alder (*Frangula alnus*), spindle (*Euonymus europaeus*), furze (*Ulex europaeus*), and bramble (*Rubus*).

Butterfly
The male upper side is lilac-blue with a narrow black line edging the wings. The fringes on the forewings are white, chequered with black, those on the hindwings are white. The underside is pale blue marked with black spots. The antennae are black, ringed and tipped with white.

The female is the same shade of blue as the male, but has broad black borders along the costa and outer margin of the forewing. These borders are wider in individuals of the second generation. The hindwing has a narrower black border with a submarginal row of black spots. There is a black discal spot on the forewing. The underside is similar to that of the male.

Variation is uncommon in this species, but sometimes occurs in the shape and size of the black spots on the underside.

Each butterfly has its own territory, which it patrols regularly, returning again and again to rest on a favourite leaf. It visits flowers and has also been observed at tree sap.

This is the only British butterfly whose main foodplant changes with the seasons: the spring eggs are laid on holly, the autumn ones on ivy.

Egg
The colour is greenish-white with a raised white network pattern and a sunken micropyle. The eggs are laid singly on the bud stems, or at the base of the calyces of the flower buds of holly or ivy, according to the season, and they hatch in about a week.

Underside

Egg on ivy; width 0·6 mm.

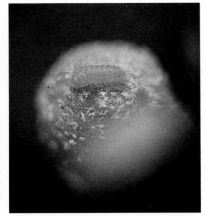

Newly hatched larva on ivy; length 0·9 mm.

Larva after second moult; length 5 mm.

Fully grown larva; length 13 mm.

Pupa; length 9 mm.

Larva

When newly emerged the head is black and the body greenish-yellow, bearing long white hairs. The colour becomes pale green after the first moult. During the third and fourth (final) instars there are three colour forms of the larva, each having a black head and short white hairs:

   (i) Yellow-green with whitish lateral lines (illustrated).
  (ii) Green with purple marks and whitish dorsal and lateral lines.
 (iii) Green with rose marks and yellowish dorsal and lateral lines.

The eggshell is not eaten on emergence. The larva feeds on the buds, eating grooves in them, and on the flowers, and when resting among them it is almost impossible to detect even with a lens. It is sluggish in its movements, rarely leaving the flower head except to moult, when it rests on a mat of silk on the back of a nearby leaf until moulting is completed. The larval stage lasts four to six weeks.

Pupa

Brown in colour with darker brown markings, it is secured by a silk girdle and by tail hooks to a silken pad attached to the underside of a convenient leaf or other support. Pupae of the first generation hatch after about two and a half weeks, while those of the second pass the winter in this stage, usually hatching during late March or April.

LYCAENIDAE **Small Copper**

♂ upper side; wingspan 32 mm.

♀ upper side; wingspan 35 mm.

BUTTERFLY
EGG
LARVA
PUPA

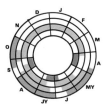

Distribution
Throughout the British Isles.

Habitat
Hillsides and downs, fields, rough ground, in fact on any open ground.

Life cycle
Three generations a year. Overwinters as a larva.

Larval foodplants
Common sorrel (*Rumex acetosa*), sheep's sorrel (*R. acetosella*), and docks (*Rumex*).

Butterfly
On the upper side, the forewing is brilliant coppery-orange marked with black spots, and with a black marginal border. The hindwing is black with a coppery-orange wavy submarginal band. On the underside the forewing is pale orange spotted with black, and the hindwing grey-brown with a red submarginal band; the antennae are black, ringed with white and tipped with orange.

The sexes are similarly marked, but females are slightly larger, and have more rounded forewings than the males.

Variation is common, and consists of changes in the ground colour, and in the extent of the black markings. One very lovely variation is ab. *caeruleopunctata*, which has a row of blue spots inside the orange band on the hindwing.

The flight of the butterfly is swift and rather difficult to follow with the eye. It is a frequent visitor to flowers, particularly bramble, marjoram, and various species of *Compositae*. Each butterfly has a territory, the focal point of which may be a tiny stone or a particular flower, from which it leaps to pursue any other passing butterfly.

Egg
The eggs are greyish-white in colour, with a raised honeycomb pattern on the surface. They are laid

Underside

Egg; width 0·6 mm.

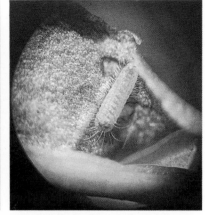

Newly hatched larva; length 1 mm.

Fully grown larva (pink and green form); length 15 mm.

Fully grown larva (green form)

Pupa; length 10 mm.

singly, usually on the upper surface of a leaf of the foodplant where the leaf blade joins the petiole, and hatch after about a week.

Larva

When newly hatched, the head is black, the body ochreous-yellow with long whitish hairs. After the first moult there are two colour forms, which remain constant until fully grown after the fourth moult. The head is olive green and the body bears very short hairs. The colour of the body may be either green or green striped with pink. Both forms match the colour of the leaves of the foodplant very closely.

The eggshell is not eaten. Directly after emergence, the larva goes to the underside of the leaf and eats out a groove in which to rest. During the early instars it perforates the leaves, thus betraying its presence. Larvae resulting from the third generation of butterflies enter into hibernation during October, on a pad of silk spun on the underside of a leaf, and remain there until the following spring. The larval stage lasts about one month in the first two generations, and about seven months in overwintering larvae.

Pupa

Pale brown in colour, marked with darker brown and black, the pupa is attached by a silken girdle and tail hooks to a pad of silk spun under a leaf or on a stem, often on the foodplant. It hatches after three to four weeks.

LYCAENIDAE **Large Copper**

♂ upper side; wingspan 40 mm.

♀ upper side; wingspan 42 mm.

BUTTERFLY
EGG
LARVA
PUPA

Distribution
Woodwalton Fen, Cambridge-shire.

Habitat
Fenland.

Life cycle
One generation a year. Over-winters as a young larva.

Larval foodplant
Great water dock (*Rumex hydro-lapathum*).

Butterfly
The male is a rich flame-red with white fringes and narrow black margins to the wings. There are two black dots on the forewing, and a row of black dots on the outer margin of the hindwing. On the underside, the forewing is orange, marked with white-ringed black spots, and with a bluish-grey marginal band. The hindwing is bluish-grey, marked with white-ringed black spots, and with an orange marginal band with black dots along each edge. The antennae are black, ringed with white and tipped with orange.

The female has a similar ground colour to the male, but is much more heavily marked with black on the upper side. The forewing has more and larger spots, and a broad black marginal band. The basal area of the hindwing is suffused with black, and there is a black marginal band with black dots. The markings on the underside are similar to those of the male.

The English Large Copper, *Lycaena dispar dispar*, fomerly lived in the fens of Cambridgeshire and Huntingdonshire, but became extinct during the 1860s, largely owing to the draining of the fens and the attentions of collectors. Several attempts were made to introduce the European subspecies *rutilus* into England and Ireland during the early part of this century, but these were unsuccessful, each colony dying out. The subspecies *batavus*, which is described here, and which very closely resembles the extinct *dispar*, was discovered in Friesland in 1915, and was introduced into Woodwalton Fen in 1927 by the Nature Conservancy Council, and it can be seen there to this day. It does not seem able to survive without assistance, as it requires its larval foodplant to be in land which is tending to dry out. Land in this condition, if left unattended, soon becomes over-grown with scrub and the foodplants choked, so careful management of the site is necessary in order to preserve the butterfly.

The flight of the Large Copper is swift, and it often basks on low vegetation. It visits flowers such as thistles and marjoram.

Eggs on great water dock

Larva after hibernation; length 6 mm.

Pair, undersides

Larva after hatching; length 1·2 mm.

Larva before third moult; length 9 mm.

Fully grown larva; length 25 mm.

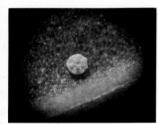
Egg; width 0·6 mm.

Larva preparing for hibernation; length 5 mm.

Pupa; length 13 mm.

Egg

The egg is greenish-white in colour, with a raised pattern and a sunken micropyle. It is laid either singly or in groups of three or four, on either surface of the foodplant leaf, sometimes scattered on the leaf blade, but more often close to the midrib. It hatches after about ten days.

Larva

Directly after emergence, the head is brownish-olive, the body pale yellow, and covered with long white hairs. After the first moult the hairs are shorter and the body green, this colouring being retained until the larva is fully grown after the third moult. During the final instar the head is greenish-ochre, the body green with darker markings, and covered with very short hairs. There is a honey gland on the tenth segment.

The eggshell is not eaten. After hatching, the larva goes to the underside of the leaf and eats out a groove in which it rests, feeding on the cuticle of the leaf. About the beginning of September, the larva assumes a pinkish hue, and enters into hibernation among dried leaves at the base of the plant. During hibernation it is capable of surviving several weeks' submergence when the fen is flooded. It begins feeding once more towards the end of March, gradually becoming green again. The larval stage lasts ten to eleven months.

Pupa

Pale brown in colour, marked with dark brown and white, the pupa is secured by a silken girdle, and by tail hooks, to a pad of silk attached to a stem of the foodplant, and is formed head downwards. It hatches after about three weeks.

♂ upper side; wingspan 33 mm.

BUTTERFLY
EGG
LARVA
PUPA

Distribution
Throughout the British Isles.

Habitat
Rough ground with shrubs.

Life cycle
One generation a year. Over-winters as a pupa.

Larval foodplants
Gorse (*Ulex europaeus*), dwarf gorse (*U. galii*), broom (*Sarothamnus scoparius*), bird's foot trefoil (*Lotus corniculatus*), rock rose (*Helianthemum chamaecistus*), dyer's green-weed (*Genista tinctoria*), whortle-berry (*Vaccinium myrtillus*), berries of buckthorn (*Rhamnus*), buds of dogwood (*Swida sanguinea*) and of bramble (*Rubus*).

Butterfly
The upper side is brown. Males have an oval area of black scent scales at the end of the discal cell on the forewing, which becomes greyish as the scent scales drop off. Females may be distinguished by the absence of this patch. The underside is green with reddish-brown margins, and a transverse row of white spots or streaks (the 'hairstreak') extending across the wings. The antennae are black and white, tipped with orange.

Variation is considerable in the extent of the white marking on the underside; the heaviest marking occurs in specimens from northern localities.

The Green Hairstreak may be found along hedgerows, on downland and heaths, the out-skirts of woods, in fact on any type of rough ground which has plenty of shrubs. It visits flowers, and takes short, swift flights, resting with closed wings on leaves, where the green colouring of the underside renders the butterfly almost invisible.

Egg
The egg is green, its surface covered with a raised white network, and with a sunken micropyle. It is

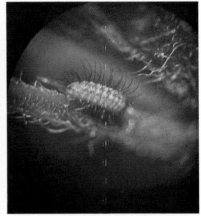

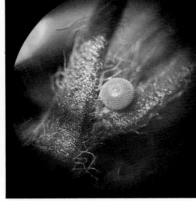

Underside

Egg; width 0·6 mm.

Larva, just hatched; length 0·9 mm.

Larva after second moult; length 8 mm.

Fully grown larva; length 15 mm.

Pupa; length 8·5 mm.

laid singly on the petals or young shoots of the various foodplants, and hatches after about a week.

Larva

When newly emerged, the head is dark brown, and the body greenish-yellow, bearing long dark hairs. After the first moult, the colour is white with brown stripes, at the second moult, green, striped with dark green and yellow, and with short hairs. Fully grown after the third moult, the head is brown, the body covered with short brown hairs. The colour is green, with oblique yellow stripes and lateral lines.

The eggshell is not eaten. The larvae feed on the flowers, berries, or young leaves of the food-plants, and are cannibalistic after the first moult. If raising this species in captivity, therefore, each larva should be kept separately. The head is very small, and is usually hidden beneath the first segment. The larval stage lasts about a month.

Pupa

Deep brown in colour, marked with black, the pupa is formed amongst the general litter underneath the foodplant, for example, under a dead fallen leaf, to which it is secured by a few threads of silk. The larval skin is retained, and the dorsal surface of the pupa is covered with very short bristles. This stage lasts for about ten months.

LYCAENIDAE **Brown Hairstreak**

♂ upper side; wingspan 38 mm.

♀ upper side; wingspan 40 mm.

BUTTERFLY
EGG
LARVA
PUPA

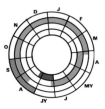

Distribution
Southern and midland counties of England, and Wales. Co. Galway and Co. Clare in Ireland.

Habitat
Bushy areas, hedgerows, and the vicinity of woods.

Life cycle
One generation a year. Over-winters as an egg.

Larval foodplant
Blackthorn (*Prunus spinosa*). In captivity, plum.

Butterfly
On the upper side the male is dark brown. At the end of the discal cell on the forewing is a black bar and a pale blotch. There are two orange marks on the hindwing at the anal angle. The underside is pale orange, marked with black lines and white stripes, and a reddish marginal band. The antennae are black and white, tipped with orange. Females are slightly larger than the males. On the upper side, instead of the pale blotch, there is an orange band. At the anal angle of the hindwing are two or three orange marks. The underside is a deeper, richer colour than that of the male, and the tails on the hindwings are usually longer.

Variation is uncommon, but sometimes takes the form of an increase in the orange markings on the upper side.

The usual haunts of this butterfly are the vicinity of woods, bushy areas, or hedgerows containing blackthorn bushes and adjacent to tall oak trees. The butterflies are seldom seen, as they spend most of their lives at the tops of oak trees, coming down only to feed or to lay eggs. They visit bramble flowers, and are active only in sunshine, when they will occasionally bask with their wings open, though normally they rest with them closed.

Egg
White in colour, with a raised honeycomb pattern on the surface, eggs are laid singly in the forks of the blackthorn twigs, usually on the smaller bushes. They remain throughout the winter, hatching during late March or early April, and are quite conspicuous on the bare twigs during the winter months.

♂ underside

♀ underside

Egg; width 0·6 mm.

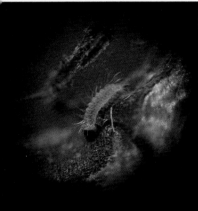

Larva, one day old; length 1 mm.   Fully grown larva; length 18 mm.   Pupa; length 12 mm.

Larva

When newly hatched, the head is black, the body pale ochre, and bearing long white hairs. After the second moult the colour becomes green with yellow markings, and this remains unchanged for the rest of the larval stage. When fully grown after the third moult, the head is blackish-brown, and the back covered with short white hairs. The colour is pale green, marked with light yellow.

The eggshell is not eaten. The larva rests on the underside of a blackthorn leaf, where its shape, colour and pattern provide a marvellous camouflage, and make it very difficult to find. The larval stage lasts about three months.

Pupa

Brown in colour, marked with darker brown, the pupa is secured by the yellowish cast larval skin, which remains adhering to a pad of silk under a leaf, or amongst the litter at the base of the foodplant. It hatches after about three weeks.

LYCAENIDAE **Purple Hairstreak**

♂ upper side; wingspan 39 mm.

♀ upper side; wingspan 37 mm.

BUTTERFLY
EGG
LARVA
PUPA

Distribution
Throughout England and Wales, and in central west Scotland. Local in Ireland.

Habitat
Oak woods.

Life cycle
One generation a year. Over-winters as an egg.

Larval foodplant
Common oak (*Quercus robur*). Has been reported on sallow (*Salix*), and Spanish chestnut (*Castanea sativa*).

Butterfly
The male is a deep purplish-blue with black outer margins to the wings, these being broader on the hindwings. The purplish-blue colour is iridescent, and its intensity varies according to the angle from which it is viewed. The underside is grey, marked with dark brown and white lines. There are two orange spots on the hindwing, one of which is black-centred, and one or two orange spots at the inner angle of the forewing. The antennae are black and white, tipped with orange, and the proboscis is yellow. The female is purplish-black

on the upper side. The discal cell and the space below it are purple. The underside is similar to that of the male.

Variation is very rare in this species. Occasionally the female may have three orange patches at the end of the cell on the forewing – this is known as ab. *flavimaculatus*.

The butterfly spends most of its time round the tops of high oaks and ashes, frequently in great numbers. The females will often come down to smaller oaks to lay their eggs. The main food seems to be honeydew left on the leaves by aphids, although the butterflies will also visit the flowers and developing fruit of brambles.

Egg
The egg is greyish-white with a raised white network and a sunken micropyle. It is laid singly on an oak twig, either close to a bud or in a fork, during July and August, and hatches the following spring.

Larva
Directly after emergence, the head is black, and the body greenish-ochre with black hairs. After the first and second moults the ground colour is darker, and the body is marked with oblique white

Underside

Egg; width 0·8 mm.

Newly emerged larva in bud; length 1·5 mm.

Larva after first moult; length 4 mm.

Half-grown larva

Fully grown larva; length 15 mm.

Pupa; length 10 mm.

stripes; the hairs are white. Fully grown after the third moult, the head is brown and very small, the body reddish-brown with short hairs. There is a white-bordered black dorsal line, and a series of dark brown and white oblique stripes on the sides.

The eggshell is not eaten. Immediately after hatching, the larva bores into the expanding buds and feeds within. During subsequent instars it rests among the old scale leaves at the bases of the opening buds, securing itself with a few strands of silk. Its colouring blends beautifully into its surroundings, making it very difficult to see. The larval stage lasts six to seven weeks.

Pupa
Reddish-brown with darker markings, the pupa may be found under moss, or among leaves, either on the ground beneath the tree, or in crevices in the trunk and larger branches. The larval skin usually remains attached, and there are a few strands of silk round the pupa, which hatches after about a month.

White Letter Hairstreak

♀ upper side; wingspan 35 mm.

Underside

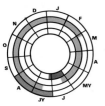

BUTTERFLY
EGG
LARVA
PUPA

Distribution
England and Wales, as far north as Yorkshire.

Habitat
The vicinity of elms.

Life cycle
One generation a year. Over-winters as an egg.

Larval foodplant
Wych elm (*Ulmus glabra*), sometimes common elm (*U. procera*).

Butterfly
The upper side of the male is blackish-brown, with a grey oval patch of scent scales at the end of the cell on the forewing. The underside is brown with a white line running across both wings, forming a distinct W towards the anal angle of the hindwing, which also has a submarginal band of black and orange markings. The antennae are black and white, tipped with orange. Females are similar to the males, but may be distinguished by the absence of the scent scale patch, and by the slightly longer tails on the hindwings.

Variation is uncommon in this species, but may take the form of an increase or decrease in the width of the white line on the underside.

The White Letter Hairstreak may be found in the vicinity of wych elms, and sometimes common elms. The butterfly is seldom seen because it flies very little, preferring to rest high up on the foliage of the elms. A stick thrown up into the branches may disturb a few, thus betraying their presence. The butterflies will come down to visit flowers, particularly bramble and privet.

Egg
The egg is button-shaped, with a sunken micropyle and a projecting rim. When first laid, the colour is green with a white rim; after about a week the egg is chocolate brown, the rim remaining white. Eggs are laid singly, usually on the underside of a twig of wych elm, sometimes under a fork, but more often along the twig at the junction of the old and the new wood, frequently on a leaf scar. The eggs remain through the winter, and hatch towards the end of February.

Larva
When newly hatched, the head is black, the body reddish-ochre and bearing black hairs. During the first and second instars, the colour darkens to a

Newly laid egg

Egg; width 0·8 mm.

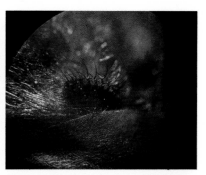

Larva, one day old; length 1·3 mm.

Larva before first moult; length 3 mm.

Larva after second moult; length 7 mm.

Fully grown larva; length 15 mm.

Fully grown larva (variegated form)

Pupa; length 9 mm.

reddish-brown. After the second moult it is green, marked with reddish brown. Fully grown after the third moult, the head is dark brown, and the body densely covered with short whitish hairs; the back is prominently ridged. The usual colouring is yellowish-green with yellowish dorsal markings and oblique white stripes on the sides, but some individuals are marked with pink.

The eggshell is not eaten. Directly after emergence, the larva goes to the opening flower buds and disappears inside. During later instars it feeds on the seeds and finally on leaves. At all stages of its life, the larva very closely resembles the various parts of the foodplant on which it is feeding. The larval stage lasts about three months.

Pupa

The pupa is brown, marked with darker lines and covered with white bristles. It is attached to a leaf or stem of the foodplant by a silken girdle and by tail hooks to a pad of silk, and hatches after about a month.

LYCAENIDAE **Black Hairstreak**

♀ upper side; wingspan 37 mm.

Underside

BUTTERFLY
EGG
LARVA
PUPA

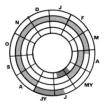

Distribution
Oxfordshire, Buckinghamshire, Huntingdonshire (Cambridge-shire), and Northamptonshire.

Habitat
Borders and rides of woods.

Life cycle
One generation a year. Over-winters as an egg.

Larval foodplant
Blackthorn (*Prunus spinosa*). In cap-tivity, plum.

Butterfly
The upper side of the male is dark brown, with a few submarginal orange marks on the hindwing. The oval patch of scent scales at the end of the cell on the forewing is indistinct. The underside is golden brown; both wings are traversed by a bluish-white line which forms a broken W near the anal angle of the hindwing. There is a sub-marginal orange band, bordered with black and white, on the hindwing, and this may extend on to the forewing. The antennae are black and white, tipped with orange. Females lack the patch of scent scales, and have more orange on the upper side, these marks extending on to the forewings.

Variation is uncommon, but may take the form of an increase in the amount of orange on the upper side.

The Black Hairstreak is a rare species which inhabits sheltered borders of woods, and rides and clearings within woods where blackthorn is present. It is a butterfly which is difficult to observe – the early stages are all extremely well camouflaged, and the adult insect is very shy and retiring, keeping mainly to the tops of oaks, and coming down only to feed from flowers such as bramble and privet, although its main food is honeydew. Females may be observed crawling about the blackthorn bushes when ovipositing.

Egg
Pale ochre in colour, the surface is covered with a raised brownish network pattern which fades during the winter, giving the egg a grey appear-ance. Eggs are laid singly on the underside of a fork of blackthorn, and large, old bushes are usu-ally chosen. They pass the winter in this stage, and hatch towards the end of March.

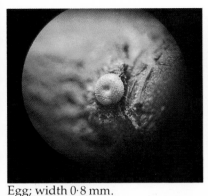
Egg; width 0·8 mm.

Larva, one day old; length 1·3 mm.

Second instar larva; length 4 mm.

Larva after second moult; length 8 mm.

Fully grown larva; length 15 mm.

Pupa; length 9·5 mm.

Larva

Just after emergence the head is black, the body brown with white hairs. After the first moult the fifth, sixth, and seventh segments are green, the remainder reddish-brown. During the next instar the brown colouring becomes more rose pink and the hairs are shorter. Fully grown after the third moult, the head is brown, the body green with oblique yellow green side stripes, and rose pink dorsal marks.

The eggshell is not eaten. The young larvae feed on the opening buds and later on the leaves. During their early stages they closely resemble the bud sheaths of the blackthorn. They are reported to be cannibalistic in captivity. The larval stage lasts about two months.

Pupa

The pupa is black and white, and bears a remarkable resemblance to a bird dropping. It is attached by tail hooks and a silken girdle to a pad of silk spun on a leaf or stem of the foodplant, and hatches after about two and a half weeks.

PIERIDAE **Wood White**

Upper side: spring brood; wingspan 42 mm.

Underside

BUTTERFLY

EGG

LARVA

PUPA

Distribution
Central, southern, and south-western counties of England south of an east-west line drawn through the Wash, and in Ireland.

Habitat
Woods, their rides and margins, and sometimes grassy areas.

Life cycle
One generation a year. In favourable years, two generations, producing butterflies in July and August. Overwinters as a pupa.

Larval foodplants
Bitter vetch (*Lathyrus montanus*), bird's foot trefoil (*Lotus corniculatus*), and various other leguminous plants.

Butterfly
The upper side of the male is white, and the forewings have black apical patches, which are smaller and blacker in the second generation. The underside is white, clouded with grey and sometimes with yellow. The antennae are black and white, tipped with orange. Females are similar to the males, but have more rounded forewings, and the black apical patch is fainter; in the second generation it may be almost absent.

Variation is usually confined to changes in the extent and intensity of the black apical patch.

The flight of this rather local species is very slow and feeble, and it is only active in sunshine. It frequently visits flowers.

Egg
Pale yellow in colour with prominent longitudinal ribs, eggs are laid singly, usually on the underside of a leaf of the foodplant, and hatch after about a week.

Larva
When newly emerged, the head and body are yellowish-ochre in colour. The body bears longitudinal rows of T-shaped spines. After the first moult these spines are less forked, and the body and head pale green with a dark green sub-dorsal line. This colouring remains unchanged until the fourth and last moult. Then the head and body are green, there is a dark green dorsal line, and a dark green and yellow spiracular stripe.

Egg; height 1 mm.

Larva, one day old; length 1·5 mm.

Fully grown larva; length 18 mm.

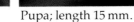

Pupa; length 15 mm.

The eggshell is partially eaten on emergence. Then the larva begins to feed on the foodplant leaves, eating notches on the edges. It is slow-moving, usually feeds by day, and rests along a leaf edge. The larval stage lasts just over a month.

Pupa

The colour is green, marked with pink. The pupa is secured by a silken girdle and tail hooks to a pad of silk spun on a stem, not usually of the food-plant, but in its vicinity. Those which produce the second generation of butterflies hatch after eight to ten days; the others remain through the winter.

PIERIDAE **Large White**

♂ upper side; wingspan 63 mm.

BUTTERFLY
EGG
LARVA
PUPA

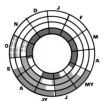

Distribution
Throughout the British Isles.

Habitat
Almost any type of country.

Life cycle
Two generations a year. In favourable years there is a partial third generation, producing butterflies in late September/October. Overwinters as a pupa.

Larval foodplants
All cruciferous plants, particularly cabbage and brussels sprouts. Also nasturtium (*Tropaeolum*) and wild mignonette (*Reseda lutea*).

side, both sexes are similar; the forewing is white with a yellow apex and two black spots, the hindwing is yellow. The antennae are black with white tips.

Variation is uncommon, but may take the form of an increase in the black markings, or the ground colour being cream.

The Large White may be found in any type of habitat, but it is particularly attracted to gardens, both for the flowers they contain, and for the cultivated species of the cabbage family on which it lays its eggs. This is classed together with the next species as 'Cabbage Whites', and they are the only butterflies in this country which cause damage to crops. Numbers of Large Whites migrate to this country every year from the Continent.

Butterfly
In both sexes the upper side is white. Males have black tips on the forewings and a black spot on the front margin of the hindwings. Females have, in addition to these markings, two black spots and a black dash on each forewing. In the spring generation all these markings are greyish. On the under-

Egg
Eggs are pale yellow when newly laid, but after a few days they become somewhat darker. Each egg has prominent longitudinal keels and fine transverse ribs. They are laid in batches, on either side of a leaf of the foodplant, and hatch after about a week.

Pieris brassicae (LINNAEUS)

♀ upper side (summer); wingspan 70 mm.

Larvae before first moult; length 3 mm.

Underside

Fully grown larva; length 40 mm.

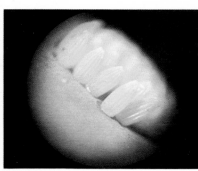

Eggs; height 1·2 mm.

Egg batch

Pupa; length 25 mm.

Larva

Directly after emergence the head is black, the body greenish-ochre in colour. Subsequent to the first moult, until fully grown after the fourth moult, the head is black and grey, the body covered with short white hairs. The ground colour is grey-green, marked with yellow and black.

Most of the eggshell is eaten. The larvae are gregarious and smell unpleasant. If disturbed, they produce droplets of dark green liquid from the mouth. The larval stage lasts about a month.

Pupa

The pupa is grey, marked with yellow and black, and is secured by a silken girdle and tail hooks. The usual site for pupation is under a ledge on a fence, under a windowsill, or a sheltered spot on the side of a wooden shed, or a tree trunk. Pupae of the first generation hatch after about a fortnight, while those which overwinter remain for about eight months.

PIERIDAE **Small White**

♂ upper side (spring); wingspan 48 mm.

♀ upper side (spring)

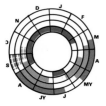

BUTTERFLY

EGG

LARVA

PUPA

Distribution
Throughout the British Isles.

Habitat
Any type of country.

Life cycle
Two generations a year; in favourable years, three, producing butterflies in September/October. Overwinters as a pupa.

Larval foodplants
All cruciferous plants, particularly cabbages. Also nasturtium (*Tropaeolum*), and wild mignonette (*Reseda lutea*).

Butterfly
The upper side is white. The male has a black tip and one black spot on the forewing, and a black spot on the inner margin of the hindwing. The female has, in addition, another black spot and a black dash on the forewing. All these markings are greyish in the spring brood, and black in the summer brood. On the underside the sexes are similar – the forewing is white with a yellow apex and two black spots, and the hindwing is yellow. The

antennae are ochreous, the clubs black with ochreous tips.

Variation is unusual. Sometimes the ground colour may be some shade of yellow – this occurs most frequently in Irish specimens.

The Small White is very common, and the resident population is reinforced each year by migrants from the Continent.

Egg
Eggs are laid singly, usually on the underside of a leaf of the foodplant. When first laid they are greenish-white, but gradually become more yellow. They are patterned with longitudinal keels and transverse ribs, and hatch in about a week.

Larva
Directly after emergence, the head is ochreous and the body yellow, with a number of short white hairs. During succeeding instars the colouring becomes greener until, when fully grown after the fourth moult, it is green with a yellow dorsal stripe and a row of yellow spots along the sides. The head is green, and the body thickly covered with short white hairs.

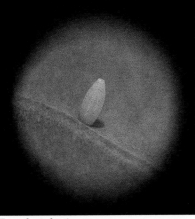

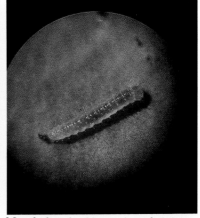

Spring brood, underside   Egg; height 1 mm.   Newly hatched larva; length 1·8 mm.

Fully grown larva; length 24 mm.   Pupa (brown form); length 19 mm.   Pupa (green form)

The eggshell is eaten. The larva is solitary, and rests in a straight position along the midrib or on a large vein of a leaf of the foodplant. Its colouring provides an excellent means of camouflage. The larval stage lasts three to four weeks.

Pupa
Attached by tail hooks and a silken girdle; the colouring varies from buff spotted with black to green marked with buff. It is found in similar situations to those chosen by the Large White, i.e., on fences, sheds, or tree trunks. Pupae of the first generation hatch after about three weeks, while overwintering ones remain for about seven months.

PIERIDAE **Green-veined White**

♂ upper side (summer); wingspan 50 mm.

BUTTERFLY ■
EGG ■
LARVA ■
PUPA ■

Distribution
Throughout the British Isles.

Habitat
Lanes, woodlands, damp meadows.

Life cycle
Two generations a year. Over-winters as a pupa.

Larval foodplants
Charlock (*Sinapis arvensis*), garlic mustard (*Alliaria petiolata*), watercress (*Nasturtium officinale*) and other cruciferous plants.

Butterfly
The upper side is white. The male has a black apex, a black spot, and black nervures on the forewing, and a black spot on the inner margin of the hindwing. Females are more heavily marked, and have an extra black spot and a black dash on the forewing. All these upper-side markings are greyish in the spring generation. The sexes are similar on the underside – the forewing is white with a yellow apex and two black spots; the hindwing is yellow, and the veins are outlined in black, giving an illusion of green. In Ireland the subspecies *britannica* occurs – this is darker in colour, particularly the females.

Variation may occur in the intensity of the markings, and in the ground colour, which is sometimes yellow.

Although a butterfly of the countryside, this species sometimes visits gardens, but does not oviposit on cultivated brassicas.

Egg
Pale yellow in colour, the eggs have longitudinal keels and fine transverse ribs. They are laid singly, usually on the underside of a leaf of the foodplant, and hatch after about five days.

Larva
When newly hatched the head is ochreous, and the body pale yellow with yellowish hairs. After

♀ upper side (spring); wingspan 50 mm.

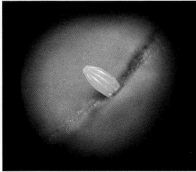

Egg; height 1 mm.

Newly hatched larva; length 1·2 mm.

Underside

Fully grown larva; length 25 mm.

Pupa (brown form); length 19 mm.

Pupa (green form)

the first moult the body is green, mottled with white. When fully grown after the fourth moult, the body is green with yellow rings round the spiracles, and the surface is covered with fine, short, white hairs.

Most of the eggshell is eaten. The larva is solitary and very well camouflaged. The larval stage lasts three to four weeks.

Pupa

Attached by tail hooks and a silken girdle to a stem or other support on or near the foodplant; the colour is very variable, and may be buff, with or without darker markings, or green marked with buff. Pupae of the first generation hatch after about a fortnight, while those of the second generation overwinter.

PIERIDAE **Orange Tip**

♂ upper side; wingspan 46 mm.

♀ upper side

BUTTERFLY ■
EGG ■
LARVA ■
PUPA ■

Distribution
England, Wales, Scotland as far north as Inverness, and in Ireland.

Habitat
Lanes and hedgerows, outskirts of woods, damp meadows.

Life cycle
One generation a year. Overwinters as a pupa.

Larval foodplants
Cruciferous plants, such as garlic mustard (*Alliaria petiolata*), hedge mustard (*Sisymbrium officinale*), cuckoo flower (*Cardamine pratensis*), charlock (*Sinapis arvensis*), watercress (*Nasturtium officinale*).

Butterfly
The upper side of the male is white, with a dusting of black scales at the bases of the wings. The forewing is tipped with black, there is a black discal spot, and the apical half of the wing is orange. The fringes are white, chequered with black. The hindwing has a grey mottling, owing to the pattern on the underside showing through. On the underside the orange patch is paler, the tips of the forewings and the whole of the hindwing mottled with greenish-yellow. This green is an optical illusion, the scales being in fact a mixture of black and yellow.

Females have a larger discal spot on the upper side, the tips of the wings are dappled with black and grey, and they lack the orange patch. On the underside, they are similar to the males except for the absence of the orange.

In Ireland, the subspecies *hibernica* occurs; this is smaller and darker than the British race, and has a tendency towards a yellow shading in the white areas of the wings.

Variation sometimes occurs in the size of the discal spot, and in the shade of the orange patch in the male. Halved gynandromorphs are found occasionally, and are very striking in appearance.

This species suffers badly from excessive trimming of roadside verges, which destroys it during the early stages.

Egg
When newly laid, the egg is greenish-white, but this changes after a day or two to deep orange. The surface is patterned with about eighteen longitudinal keels, connected by fine transverse ribs. The eggs are laid singly among the flower heads of the foodplants, either on the flower stalks or on the calyces, and they hatch after about a week.

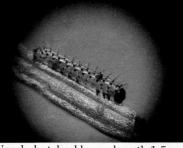

Newly hatched larva; length 1·5 mm.

♂ underside

Larva before second moult; length 6 mm.

Pupa (green form); length 23 mm.

Egg; height 1·2 mm.

Fully grown larva; length 30 mm.

Pupae (brown form)

Larva

Directly after emergence the head is shining black, the body pale orange with short black spines. During the next instar, the body becomes greener, with a white lateral line. After the fourth and last moult, the head and body are bluish-green, shading into white on the sides, and dark green on the ventral surface. The whole surface bears short black or white bristles.

The eggshell is eaten. During the early instars, the larvae are cannibalistic. They feed on the seedpods of the foodplants, and are very well camouflaged in all instars. The larval stage lasts about a month.

Pupa

The usual colour is pale brown, but some may be green, thus retaining the colour of the newly formed pupa. The pupa is attached by tail hooks and a silken girdle to a stem, not usually on the foodplant. The pupal stage lasts throughout the winter.

PIERIDAE **Clouded Yellow**

Upper sides: ♂, ♀ and ♀ *helice*;
wingspan ♂ 57 mm., ♀ 62 mm.

♂ underside

BUTTERFLY
EGG
LARVA
PUPA

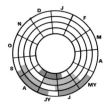

Distribution
A migrant, it reaches all parts of the British Isles, but is most common in the south.

Habitat
Rough ground and hillsides, and particularly clover and lucerne fields.

Life cycle
One generation a year from migrant parents – it cannot survive our winter.

Larval foodplants
Leguminous plants, mainly clover (*Trifolium*), lucerne (*Medicago sativa*), trefoil (*Lotus*).

Butterfly
The male is orange with black marginal bands on both fore and hindwings. The forewing has a black discal spot, and there is a deep orange spot in the centre of the hindwing. The underside is deep yellow; the forewing has a black discal spot, and in the centre of the hindwing is a metallic silver spot circled with red-brown and shaped like a figure eight. The fringes, legs, and antennae are pink.

There are two colour forms of the female. One – the more common – is similar to the male except for the presence of yellow spots in the black borders. The second – f. *helice* – is similarly marked, but the ground colour of the wings is pale primrose yellow or whitish.

Variation occurs frequently in the amount of yellow spotting on the females, and in the ground colour, which may range through many shades of yellow to white.

The Clouded Yellow does not rest with its wings open. It visits flowers, and its flight is extremely strong and rapid. A migrant from southern Europe, it cannot survive our winters, and the adults or the early stages are killed by the onset of cold weather.

♀ *helice*, underside

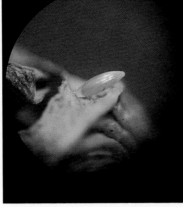

Egg; height 1·1 mm.

Larva after first moult; length 3 mm.

Larva after second moult; length 9 mm.

Fully grown larva; length 33 mm.

Pupa; length 22 mm.

Egg

The egg is marked with fine transverse ribs running between about twenty longitudinal keels. When first laid it is yellowish-white, but after two days it becomes a rich pink. Eggs are laid singly on the upper surface of a leaf of the foodplant, and hatch after about a week.

Larva

Directly after emergence the head is black, the body greenish-yellow, and covered with very short whitish bristles. After the first moult, the larva is grey-green with a darker head. After the second moult, the colour of the body is a clear green with a white lateral line. When fully grown after the fourth moult, the head and body are green, covered with short white hairs. The spiracular line is white and yellow, spotted with pink.

Most of the eggshell is eaten. At first, the larva feeds only on the cuticle of the leaf, but later perforates it, and finally eats the whole leaf. During each instar, the colouring of the larva matches that of the foodplant leaves, making it difficult to see. The larval stage lasts about a month.

Pupa

Yellowish-green in colour, marked with a few black dots, the pupa is secured to a stem, either on the foodplant or near by, by tail hooks and a silken girdle, and it hatches after about two and a half weeks.

PIERIDAE **Brimstone**

Upper sides: ♂ *above*, ♀ *below*; wingspan 58 mm.

♂ underside

BUTTERFLY ▣
EGG ▣
LARVA ▣
PUPA ▣

Distribution
England and Wales, south of the Lake District, and in Ireland.

Habitat
Open woodland or rough bushy land where its foodplants grow.

Life cycle
One generation a year. Over-winters as a butterfly.

Larval foodplants
Buckthorn (*Rhamnus catharticus*), alder buckthorn (*Frangula alnus*).

Butterfly
The upper side of the male is bright sulphur yellow with an orange spot in the centre of each wing, and reddish spots at the ends of the veins and along the front margin of the forewing towards the apex. The colouring of the underside is duller, and the spots are chocolate brown. The antennae are pink, and the thorax is covered with silky white hair. The wing shape is unique among British butterflies.

Females are similarly marked to the males, but the ground colour is pale greenish-yellow.

Variation is very rare in this species, but occasionally specimens are reported with orange or red patches on the wings.

The Brimstone does not rest with its wings open. It is a frequent visitor to flowers. It hibernates as a butterfly, usually among evergreens, and will emerge for a short flight on warm days during the autumn. It was known to the early entomologists as the 'butter-coloured fly', and it is thought that the contraction of this name gave us the word 'butterfly'.

Egg
Eggs are laid singly, usually on the underside of a young leaf or on a terminal shoot of the foodplant. When first laid, they are greenish-white, becoming yellow after two or three days. There are ten longitudinal keels, connected by fine transverse ribs. The eggs are not always symmetrical, so some appear to be somewhat banana-shaped. They hatch after about ten days.

Larva
When newly hatched, the head and body are yellow with short white hairs. After the first and second moults, the ground colour is green. Subse-

Newly hatched larva; length 1·7 mm. Fully grown larva; length 33 mm.

♀ underside

Egg; height 1·3 mm. Larva after third moult; length 19 mm. Pupa; length 22·5 mm.

quent to the third and fourth (final) moults, the body is green, becoming bluish-green on the sides, with a white spiracular stripe, the whole surface being covered with very small white bristles.

The eggshell is not eaten. The larva rests in a straight position on the upper side of a leaf of the foodplant, along the midrib, and its presence can be detected by the pieces eaten out of the leaf. The larval stage lasts about a month.

Pupa
Pale green in colour, faintly marked with darker green and purple, the pupa is attached by tail hooks and a silken girdle to a stem, not necessarily of the foodplant. It hatches after about a fortnight.

PAPILIONIDAE **Swallowtail**

♂ upper side; wingspan 80 mm.

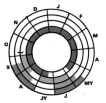

BUTTERFLY
EGG
LARVA
PUPA

Distribution
A few fens of Suffolk, Cambridge-shire, and the Norfolk Broads.

Habitat
Fens and broads.

Life cycle
One or two generations a year. Overwinters as a pupa.

Larval foodplants
Milk parsley (*Peucedanum palustre*), angelica (*Angelica sylvestris*), wild carrot (*Daucus carota*), fennel (*Foeniculum vulgare*), and other species of *Umbelliferae*. In captivity, the leaves of cultivated carrot.

Butterfly
The upper side is yellow, marked with black, blue, and red. The markings on the underside are similar, but the black is thickly dusted with yellow scales. The abdomen is black and yellow, and the antennae black. The sexes are similar, females being slightly larger, but the males may be distinguished easily by the presence of prominent claspers at the tip of the abdomen.

Variation is uncommon, but occasionally takes the form of an increase or decrease in the amount of black marking.

The habitat of the Swallowtail in this country is fenland, though continental races may be found in many types of country, including mountainsides. The British race is known as ssp. *britannicus*, and has broader black markings than other European races. The butterflies visit flowers, and often flutter their wings while feeding. Their flight is rather slow, and they are not very spectacular in flight, in spite of being the largest British butterfly.

Egg
The eggs are laid singly on the leaflets of the food-plant, and at first are pale yellow, but after a day or so develop brown markings. The surface is smooth, and they hatch after about a week.

Larva
Directly after emergence the head is black, the body grey-black, marked dorsally with white, and bearing short black spines. This colouring re-

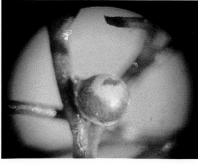

Egg; height 0·9 mm.

Larva before first moult; length 7 mm.

Underside

Larva after third moult; length 22 mm.

Larva after fourth moult; Fully grown larva length 41 mm.   Pupa (green form)   Pupa (brown form); length 29 mm.

mains, becoming more pronounced, until after the third moult, when it is white, marked with black and with orange spots on the sides. When fully grown after the fourth moult, the head is yellow-green and black, and the body green with an orange-spotted black band round each segment. Behind the head is a pair of soft orange horns (the osmeterium), normally hidden, which are extruded when the larva is alarmed, and which give off an unpleasant smell.

Most of the eggshell is eaten. During the first three instars, the larva closely resembles a bird dropping. It is solitary, and feeds by day. The larval stage lasts about a month.

Pupa
Pupae are variable in colour, ranging from greenish-yellow to pale brown marked with black. They are attached by tail hooks and a silken girdle, either to a reed stem, or to the foodplant. Those which do not overwinter hatch in two to three weeks.

HESPERIIDAE **Dingy Skipper**

Upper side; wingspan 29 mm.

BUTTERFLY

EGG

LARVA

PUPA

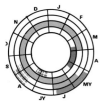

Distribution
England and Wales, parts of Scotland, and in Ireland.

Habitat
Rough ground and hillsides, particularly chalk and limestone.

Life cycle
One generation a year. In favourable years in the south, two, giving butterflies in August. Overwinters as a fully grown larva.

Larval foodplant
Bird's foot trefoil (*Lotus corniculatus*).

Butterfly
The upper side is fuscous brown, marked with darker brown and white. The fringes are grey, chequered with brown. The underside is golden brown with a few white dots, and the antennae are black, ringed with white. The sexes are similar but males have a fold on the basal area of the forewing costa containing a pocket of scent scales.

Variation does occur, mainly in the shade of the ground colour. In Ireland, this species is represented in Co. Clare by the ssp. *baynesi*, which has a darker ground colour and paler markings.

The flight is swift, and the butterfly often basks on the ground with its wings open. It roosts for the night on a grass head or a dead flower head with its wings laid along its body like a noctuid moth.

Egg
The egg has twelve to thirteen prominent keels, and when newly laid is yellow, but after a few days it becomes orange. It is laid singly on the upper side of a leaf of the foodplant, and hatches after about a fortnight.

Larva
When newly hatched the head is black, the body yellow, with a dark brown band on the first seg-

Underside

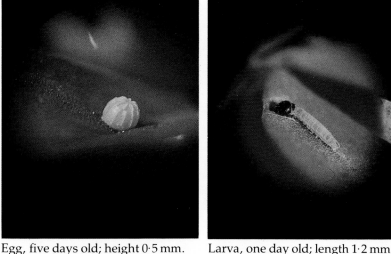

Egg, five days old; height 0·5 mm.

Larva, one day old; length 1·2 mm.

Fully grown larva; length 17·5 mm.

Hibernaculum

Pupa; length 14 mm.

ment. After the first moult the body becomes green, and this remains unchanged until fully grown after the fourth moult, when the head is purplish-black, and the body green with a dark green dorsal stripe.

The eggshell is not eaten. The larva spins a few of the foodplant leaves together with silk to form a tent, inside which it lives. It moves about only at night, and therefore is difficult to observe. At the end of July or the beginning of August, it constructs a more substantial hibernaculum, in which it remains, fully grown, until it pupates the following May. The larval stage lasts about ten months.

Pupa
The thorax and wingcases are dark green, and the abdomen chestnut brown. The pupa is attached by tail hooks inside the cocoon-like structure of the hibernaculum, and hatches after about a month.

HESPERIIDAE **Grizzled Skipper**

Upper side; wingspan 27 mm.

BUTTERFLY

EGG

LARVA

PUPA

Distribution
England, as far north as south Yorkshire, and Wales.

Habitat
Rough ground and hillsides, meadows, and open areas in woods.

Life cycle
One generation a year. In favourable years, two, producing butterflies in August. Overwinters as a pupa.

Larval foodplants
Barren strawberry (*Potentilla sterilis*), wild strawberry (*Fragaria visca*), creeping cinquefoil (*Potentilla reptans*), bramble (*Rubus*), raspberry (*Rubus idaeus*).

Butterfly
The upper side is black, patterned with white; the fringes are white, chequered with black. The underside of the forewing is similar to the upper side, but the hindwing is brown, patterned with white. The antennae are black and white, tipped with orange. The sexes are similar, but the male has a fold covering a patch of scent scales on the forewing, similar to that of the Dingy Skipper.

Variation is frequent in the extent of the white markings.

The flight is very swift and difficult to follow with the eye. The butterfly frequently basks in the sun with its wings open flat.

Egg
The egg has about twenty longitudinal keels, and when first laid it is greenish in colour, this gradually fading to white. It is laid singly, on either surface of a leaf of the foodplant, and hatches after about ten days.

Larva
Directly after emergence the head is black and the body pale ochre, with a black collar mark on the first segment. After the first and second moults the body is covered with very short white hairs and is yellow with brown markings. After the

Underside

Egg; height 0·5 mm.

Larval home

Larva after second moult; length 6·5 mm.

Fully grown larva; length 16 mm.

Larva spinning cocoon

Pupa (removed from cocoon); length 12·5 mm.

Cocoon

third moult the colouring is similar, with the addition of a brown dorsal line. When fully grown after the fourth moult, the head is black, the body green with darker brown stripes, and shading to pink on the dorsal surface – when about to pupate, the pink colour is much more pronounced.

The eggshell is not eaten. During the first two instars, the larva lives under a web of silk on the upper side of a leaf of the foodplant. Subsequent to the second moult, it draws the edges of the leaves together to form a tent. The larval stage lasts about two months.

Pupa

The pupa is reddish-brown with pearly white wingcases. It is formed inside a loose cocoon among the basal stems of the foodplant, and is held securely in the cocoon by the bristles which cover the head and dorsal surface, and by tail hooks. This stage lasts about nine months.

♂ upper side; wingspan 29 mm.

BUTTERFLY
EGG
LARVA
PUPA

Distribution
In England – formerly local in central and eastern counties, e.g., Cambridgeshire and Leicestershire, but now possibly extinct.

In Scotland – western Scotland, especially Inverness-shire.

Habitat
Clearings in woods.

Life cycle
One generation a year. Overwinters as a fully grown larva.

Larval foodplants
Bromus spp., particularly wood false brome (*Brachypodium sylvaticum*), and purple moor grass (*Molinia caerulea*).

Butterfly
The upper side is blackish-brown, dusted with yellow scales, and marked with orange-yellow spots. The underside is similarly marked, but the ground colour is much more yellow. The black clubs of the antennae are tipped with orange. The sexes are similar, the female being slightly larger, the wings more rounded, and the spots paler than in the male.

Variation, which occurs fairly frequently, consists mainly of an increase or decrease in the number and size of the spots.

The haunts of this butterfly in England were glades and rides in deciduous woodlands. In Scotland it occurs in clearings in mixed woodland, sometimes on slopes, and near streams or lochs. The flight is swift, but the butterfly will bask on grasses, bracken, and bog myrtle with outspread wings. At the approach of rain it descends deep

♀ upper side; wingspan 31 mm.

into the grass tussocks. It frequently visits flowers such as bugle and heath spotted orchid.

Egg

The egg is pearly white in colour, and the surface has a faint pattern of very fine reticulations. It is laid singly on a grass blade, and hatches after about ten days.

Larva

When newly emerged, the head is black, the body yellowish-white with a black collar on the first segment. After the first moult, the body is yellowish-green, still with the black collar. After the second moult, the body is pale green marked with darker lines, the collar is replaced by a black spot, and there is a black mark on the last segment. Subsequent to the third skin change, the body is pale green with dark green and white lines. The two black marks mentioned in the previous instar are still present, and the head is brown and black. When fully grown after the fourth moult, the head is pale green and the body green, marked with dark green and white lines, but completely lacking the two black spots. Six to seven weeks after the final moult, the head and body of the larva become pale yellow; it then hibernates, and when it emerges from hibernation it is pinkish-buff with darker lines.

On emergence, just over half the eggshell is consumed. The larva then constructs a tube by drawing together the edges of a grass blade with silk, and in this it lives, emerging to feed on the blade, eventually leaving only its home supported on the midrib of the blade. It hibernates in a shelter made by drawing together several blades with silk; this is constructed during early October, and the larva emerges from it the following March.

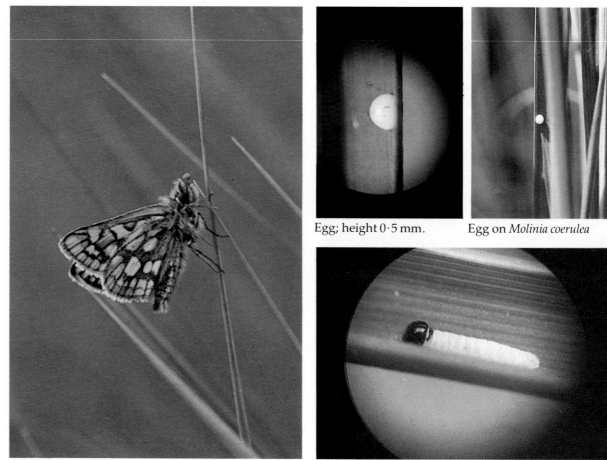

Egg; height 0·5 mm.   Egg on *Molinia coerulea*

♂ underside   Larva, one day old; length 2 mm.

After hibernation, no attempt is made to feed, the larva resting on the grass blades for up to a week before pupating. The larval stage lasts about ten months.

Pupa
Pale buff in colour, marked with darker lines, the pupa very closely resembles a piece of dead, withered grass. It is attached by tail hooks and a girdle to a mat of silk inside a shelter formed by drawing together several dead grass blades. This stage lasts five to six weeks.

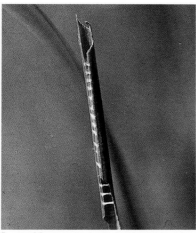

Larval home in early instar

Larva after first moult; length 6 mm.

Larva after second moult; length 10 mm.

Larva after third moult; length 18 mm.

Fully grown larva; length 23 mm.

Larva before hibernation

Hibernaculum

Larva leaving hibernaculum

Pupa; length 15 mm.

HESPERIIDAE **Small Skipper**

♂ upper side; wingspan 30 mm.

♀ upper side; wingspan 30 mm.

BUTTERFLY
EGG
LARVA
PUPA

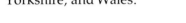

Distribution
Most of England as far north as Yorkshire, and Wales.

Habitat
Grassy areas.

Life cycle
One generation a year. Over-winters as a newly hatched larva.

Larval foodplants
The softer grasses, such as Yorkshire fog (*Holcus lanatus*), cat's tail (*Phleum pratense*), soft grass (*Holcus mollis*), wood false brome (*Brachypodium sylvaticum*).

Butterfly
The upper side of the wings is orange-brown. The veins are black near the margins, which are bordered with black. The antennae are black above and orange below – the undersides of the clubs are reddish-orange. The underside of the wings is pale orange-brown with an olive tint on the hindwings. The sexes may be distinguished readily by the presence in the male of an oblique black bar of scent scales on the forewing.

Variation is uncommon, but may take the form of changes in the shade of the ground colour.

The Small Skipper may be found on waste ground, on hillsides, meadows, and the rides and edges of woods, often in damp areas. The flight is swift, and the butterfly is greatly attracted to flowers. When basking it adopts a typical 'Skipper' attitude – the forewings half open, the hindwings fully open and flat.

Egg
The eggs are whitish in colour and have no clearly visible surface features. When ovipositing, the female settles on a grass stem, inserts the tip of her abdomen inside the grass sheath, and lays a number of eggs in a row inside the sheath. The eggs are not very firmly attached, and will fall out of the sheath on the least disturbance. They hatch after about three weeks.

Larva
Directly after emergence, the head is brown marked with black, and the body pale yellow with a brown collar mark on the first segment. After the first moult the body becomes greenish-ochre with darker green and white lines, and the collar disappears. When fully grown after the fourth moult, the head is green, the body paler green with darker lines and a white subspiracular stripe.

The eggshell is eaten on emergence. The larva then spins a small dense cocoon inside the grass

Underside

Egg laying in grass sheath

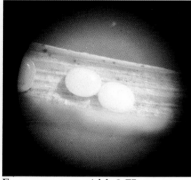
Eggs; greatest width 0·75 mm.

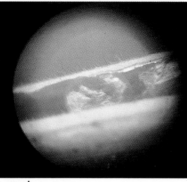
Larval cocoons

First instar larva after hibernation; length 3 mm.

Fully grown larva; length 21 mm.

Pupal cocoon

Pupa (removed from cocoon); length 18 mm.

sheath in which it spends the winter, emerging during April, when it constructs a tube by pulling together the edges of a grass blade with silk, and lives in a succession of these structures until the last instar, when it rests on a blade in the open. The larval stage lasts ten to eleven months.

Pupa

The pupa is green, the tongue case ochreous, the 'beak' on the head and the cremaster are lilac pink. It is attached by tail hooks and a girdle inside a coarse cocoon spun amongst the grass stems or blades, and hatches after about three weeks.

♂ upper side; wingspan 27 mm.

Underside

BUTTERFLY
EGG
LARVA
PUPA

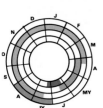

Distribution
Southern and south-eastern counties of England.

Habitat
Waste ground, hillsides, meadows, and the rides and edges of woods.

Life cycle
One generation a year. Overwinters as an egg.

Larval foodplants
Grasses, such as couch (*Agropyron repens*), cat's tail (*Phleum pratense*), and brome (*Brachypodium*).

Butterfly
The upper side is orange-brown and the margins are bordered with black. The underside is pale orange-brown with an olive tint on the hindwings. This species is almost identical to the Small Skipper, but may be distinguished from it by the following features: in the Essex Skipper, the undersides of the clubs of the antennae are black, and in the male, the black bar of scent scales is less oblique and shorter.

Variation sometimes occurs in the shade of the ground colour.

The habitats of the Essex Skipper are similar to those of the Small Skipper, and the two species often fly together, sharing the same liking for flowers.

Egg
The eggs are dull white with no apparent surface features. They are deposited inside a grass sheath, in a row, in a similar manner to those of the Small Skipper, but do not hatch until the following spring.

Larva
When just emerged, the head is black, the body pale yellow with a dark brown collar on the first segment. During succeeding instars the body becomes greener, with darker stripes. Fully grown after the fourth moult, the head is pale brown, the

Antennae – showing black tips on underside

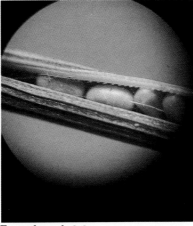

Eggs; length 0·8 mm.

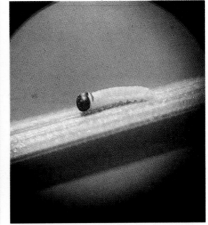

Larva, one day old; length 1·6 mm.

Fully grown larva; length 22 mm.

Cocoon

Pupa; length 15 mm.

body pale green with darker green and white stripes.

The eggshell is not eaten. The larva lives in a tube formed from the grass blades until the final instar, when it rests on the open blades, feeding both by day and night. The larval stage lasts from two to two and a half months.

Pupa

Yellowish-green in colour, with the beak and cremaster white, the pupa is secured by tail hooks and a girdle inside a coarse cocoon spun low down among the grass stems or blades, and hatches after about three weeks.

♂ upper side; wingspan 25 mm.

♀ upper side; wingspan 27 mm.

BUTTERFLY
EGG
LARVA
PUPA

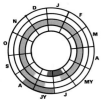

Distribution
The coast of Dorset from Swanage westward to Devon.

Habitat
Grassy slopes and cliffs.

Life cycle
One generation a year. Over-winters as a newly hatched larva.

Larval foodplants
Grasses, such as chalk false brome (*Brachypodium pinnatum*), and couch (*Agropyron repens*).

Butterfly
The upper side of the male is olive brown in colour, with black margins. On the forewing there is a faint ring of lighter brown spots, and a black bar of scent scales. The underside is golden brown, and the antennae are black and white, tipped with orange. The female is slightly larger than the male, she lacks the black scent scales, and the circle of pale spots on the forewing is much more distinct.

Variation is very uncommon. Two halved gynandromorphs have been recorded.

The Lulworth Skipper occurs on grassy slopes, usually south-facing, but its main habitats are coastal cliffs. It flies strongly and very swiftly, and is a frequent visitor to flowers.

Egg
The eggs, which have no obvious surface features, are a pale yellowish-white until shortly before hatching, when the black head of the larva becomes clearly visible through the shell. They are laid in rows inside the grass sheaths, and hatch after about three weeks.

Larva
Immediately after emergence the head is black, the body pale yellow with a dark brown collar mark on the first segment. After the first moult, this collar disappears, and the body is greenish-yellow with a dark green dorsal line. From the next skin change until the larva is fully grown after the fourth moult, the head is greenish-buff, the body green, striped with dark green and yellowish-white.

The eggshell is not eaten. After hatching, and without attempting to feed, the larva spins a

♂ underside

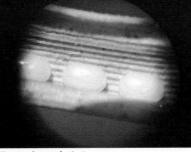

Eggs; length 1·6 mm.

Eggs in grass sheath

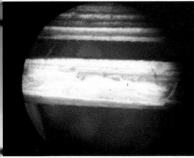

Larval cocoons

Larva after third moult; length 13 mm.

Larval tube

Fully grown larva; length 24 mm.

Pupal cocoon

Pupa; length 18 mm.

dense white cocoon inside the grass sheath in which it hibernates until the following April. It then emerges from its hibernaculum, and the members of the group disperse, each taking up a position on a grass blade, and spinning the edges together with silk to form a tube in which it lives, emerging to feed. During the last instar, it dispenses with the tube and rests on a blade in the open. The larval stage lasts ten to eleven months.

Pupa
The colouring is whitish-green, striped with white, the beak on the head often being tinged with pink. The pupa is concealed in a very loose cocoon low down among the grasses, and is secured by tail hooks and a silk girdle. It may be either head up or head down, and hatches after about a fortnight.

♂ upper side; wingspan 31 mm.

♀ upper side; wingspan 36 mm.

BUTTERFLY
EGG
LARVA
PUPA

Distribution
Confined to chalk hills in the south of England.

Habitat
Chalk hills and downs with short turf.

Life cycle
One generation a year. Over-winters as an egg.

Larval foodplants
Grasses, mainly sheep's fescue (*Festuca ovina*).

Butterfly
The male is dark olive brown on the upper side, and the wings are patterned with amber yellow spots. On the forewing is a conspicuous black bar of scent scales. The underside is yellowish-green, marked with silvery spots. The antennae are black and white, tipped with orange. The female is similarly marked, but is larger than the male, her wings are more rounded, she lacks the black bar on the forewing, and the yellow spots are brighter.

Variation is uncommon, but occasionally the ground colour may vary slightly.

The Silver-spotted Skipper is now quite rare, and very restricted in its range. The flight is swift, but the butterfly frequently settles on the short turf, particularly on anthills. It eagerly visits flowers such as ground thistles, scabious, and hawkbit.

Egg
The egg, which is whitish in colour, has no prominent surface features, and in shape closely resembles an upside-down pudding basin. It is laid singly on a grass blade, fairly low down on the plant, and passes the winter before hatching during February or March.

Larva
When newly emerged the head is black, the body deep yellow with a dark brown collar mark on the first segment. The body colouring gradually takes on a more greenish hue until after the third moult, when it is olive green. After the fourth moult, fully grown, the head is blackish-brown, the body olive green, with the black collar still present on the first segment.

The eggshell is not eaten. The larva is solitary, and spins several grass blades together to form a

♂ underside   ♀ underside

Egg; height 0·7 mm.   Larva, one day old; length 2 mm.   Larva after third moult; length 19 mm.

Fully grown larva; length 26 mm.   Pupa; length 19 mm.

tent in which it lives. This structure is usually situated towards the base of the plant. The larval stage lasts three to four months.

Pupa

The head, thorax, and wingcases are blackish-green, the abdomen brownish-olive, and the whole surface is covered with short bristles, those on the head being hooked. The pupa is enclosed in a strong coarse cocoon, reinforced with pieces of chewed-off grass, among the grass stems close to the ground. It is secured by tail hooks and the hooked bristles on the head, and hatches after about ten days.

HESPERIIDAE **Large Skipper**

♂ upper side; wingspan 33 mm.

BUTTERFLY
EGG
LARVA
PUPA

Distribution
England, Wales, and parts of southern Scotland.

Habitat
Meadows, rough ground, hillsides, the edges, rides, and clearings in woods, and coastal cliffs.

Life cycle
One generation a year. Overwinters as a larva.

Larval foodplants
Cock's foot grass (*Dactylis glomerata*), and wood false brome (*Brachypodium sylvaticum*). In captivity, other grasses.

Butterfly
The upper side of the male is brown shaded with orange-brown and marked with orange spots. On the forewing is a very conspicuous black scent scale mark. The underside is orange-brown, shaded with green, the pattern of spots being paler than on the upper side. The antennae are black and orange. Females are slightly larger than males, they lack the patch of scent scales, and the pattern of spots is more clearly defined.

Variation is uncommon, but the ground colour sometimes varies. A halved gynandromorph was caught in 1944 in south Wales and is now in the national collection, and another was bred by the author in 1974.

The flight of the Large Skipper is swift and strong, and it frequents flowers.

Egg
The surface of the egg has a very fine reticulation, but to the unaided eye it appears smooth. The colour when laid is white, but this gradually becomes pale yellow, and shortly before hatching, the larva's black head shows through the shell. Eggs are laid singly on the underside of a grass blade, and hatch after about two and a half weeks.

Larva
Directly after emergence the head is black, and the body primrose yellow with a black collar on the

♀ upper side; wingspan 35 mm.　　Newly hatched larva; length 2·5 mm.　Hibernaculum

Egg; width 0·8 mm.

Underside　　　　　Fully grown larva; length 28 mm.　Pupa; length 19 mm.

first segment. Subsequent to the first moult, the body gradually becomes greener. The head is brown after the third moult, and the collar disappears at the fourth moult. The larva is fully grown after the sixth moult, and then the head is brownish-black, the body bluish-green with a dark green dorsal stripe and a cream-coloured spiracular line.

The eggshell is eaten. The young larva constructs a tube in which to live by pulling together the edges of a grass blade with strands of silk. During September, after the fourth moult, it constructs a hibernaculum by fastening together several blades with silk, and it remains in this until the following March. The larval stage lasts ten to eleven months.

Pupa

The head, thorax, and wingcases are black with a grey bloom, and the abdomen is greenish-grey. The whole surface is covered with short bristles. The pupa is enclosed in a cocoon spun inside a tent formed by several grass blades, and it is secured by tail hooks and the bristles on the head. It hatches after about three weeks.

Rare Migrants

The ten species mentioned in this section are rare and infrequent visitors to this country – in good years, some specimens of most of them are reported here, in other years, only scattered individuals. A brief description of the butterfly is given, together with its time of appearance and larval foodplants.

Danaidae Monarch *or* Milkweed Butterfly – *Danaus plexippus* (Linnaeus)

The upper side is chestnut brown with black veins; the margins have broad black borders containing two rows of white spots. The apical area of the forewing is patterned with amber and white spots. The male has an oval patch of black scent scales on the second median vein of the hindwing, which is absent in the female. The underside is similar. The antennae are black, and the head, thorax and abdomen are black with white spots. The size and pattern of this butterfly make it unmistakable.

The Monarch is established in North America, where it is a famous migrant, and in the Canary Islands, where it appears to be static, but it is possible that the few individuals which are reported in this country may originate from there.

Most of the British records are from the south and west, from August to October. The larval foodplants, milkweeds (*Asclepias*) are not indigenous to this country.

Monarch: ♀ upper side; wingspan 110 mm.

Nymphalidae Queen of Spain Fritillary – *Argynnis lathonia* (Linnaeus)

The upper side is orange-brown, spotted with black. The large silver spots on the underside of the hindwings will prevent confusion with our resident Fritillaries.

The Queen of Spain Fritillary is common in southern Europe. It has been found in the south and east of England from May onwards. The larval foodplants are *Viola* spp., and the butterfly may breed here occasionally, but it cannot survive our winters.

Queen of Spain Fritillary: upper side and underside; wingspan ♂ 46 mm., ♀ 52 mm.

Nymphalidae Camberwell Beauty – *Nymphalis antiopa* (Linnaeus)

The upper side of the wings is chocolate brown with a straw-coloured margin – just inside this border is a line of pale blue spots. The underside is similar, but without the blue spots.

The English name derives from the fact that the first British specimen was taken at Camberwell in 1748. The butterfly is common in Scandinavia and Germany, and these areas are probably the source of our migrants, which are usually found in the east of the British Isles, and along the south coast. Most sightings occur in August and September, although sometimes butterflies are seen in the spring; these may have hibernated here. The species is not thought to breed in this country, although its foodplants are willow, elm, sallow, and birch.

Camberwell Beauty: upper side; wingspan ♂ 74 mm., ♀ 84 mm.

Lycaenidae Long-tailed Blue – *Lampides boeticus* (Linnaeus)

The upper side of the male is purplish-blue. At the anal angle of the hindwing are two black spots and a short, black, white-tipped tail. Females are brownish-black, similarly marked, with the bases of the wings shaded blue. The best identification for this species is given by the underside – pale brown marked with white lines, and with two metallic-ringed black spots at the base of the tail.

This is one of the most widely distributed species in the world. Its nearest habitats to this country are the Mediterranean countries. Here, it is a very rare visitor, but occasionally reaches us in July. It may breed here, but cannot survive the winter. The larval foodplants are various leguminous plants, particularly everlasting pea (*Lathyrus latifolius*).

Long-tailed Blue: underside; wingspan ♂ 34 mm., ♀ 36 mm.

Lycaenidae Short-tailed Blue – *Everes argiades* (Pallas)

The male is violet blue with short tails, the female brown shaded with violet blue at the bases of the wings. At the anal angle of the hindwing, the female has black spots edged with orange at the base of the tail. The underside is very similar to that of the Holly Blue, but may be distinguished by the presence of three orange spots near the anal angle of the hindwing.

This is probably our rarest migrant, and has been reported very few times. It is resident in France, and British records are for July and August. The larval foodplant is bird's foot trefoil (*Lotus corniculatus*). In 1885, several specimens were taken at Bloxworth in Dorset, and the species is sometimes referred to as the Bloxworth Blue.

Short-tailed Blue: upper sides – ♀ *left,* ♂ *right;* wingspan ♀ 25 mm., ♂ 23 mm.

Lycaenidae Mazarine Blue – *Cyaniris semiargus* (Rottemburg)

The male is purplish-blue with a narrow black outer margin and white fringes, the female dark brown with no trace of blue. The underside bears some resemblance to that of the Large Blue, but there are fewer spots.

The Mazarine Blue was formerly resident in Britain, but became extinct during the early part of this century. It is common in Europe, and occasional specimens are reported here, usually in the south during June or July. The larval foodplants are red clover (*Trifolium pratense*), kidney vetch (*Anthyllis vulneraria*), and other leguminous plants.

Mazarine Blue: ♂ upper side; wingspan 36 mm.

Mazarine Blue: ♀ upper side; wingspan 36 mm.

Mazarine Blue: underside

Pieridae Black-veined White – *Aporia crataegi* (Linnaeus)

The wings are white with black veins. Females look rather more transparent, as their wings are less densely scaled than those of the males.

This species is another former resident of this country which became extinct during the 1920s. It is still widespread on the Continent, so it is possible that stray specimens may reach us occasionally. It is on the wing in June and July, and the larval foodplants are hawthorn (*Crataegus monogyna*), blackthorn (*Prunus spinosa*), and cultivated fruit trees.

Black-veined White: underside; wingspan 72 mm.

Pieridae Bath White – *Pontia daplidice* (Linnaeus)

The Bath White can be confused very easily with the female Orange Tip – the points of difference are:

(i) The black apical patch on the Bath White has white spots in it.

(ii) The black discal spot is larger than that of the Orange Tip, and has white in it.

(iii) The underside of the hindwing of the Bath White is much greener than that of the Orange Tip.

Bath Whites are found in many parts of Europe, particularly the southern areas, but here it is a very rare visitor. Most records are from the southern counties during July and August. The larva feeds on wild mignonette (*Reseda lutea*).

Bath White: upper side and underside; wingspan 50 mm.

Pieridae Pale Clouded Yellow –*Colias hyale* (Linnaeus)

The upper side of the male is primrose yellow. The outer margin of the forewing and the apex is black with a row of yellow spots, and in the centre of the forewing is a black spot. The hindwings are narrowly bordered with black, and the central spot is orange. Females are similarly marked, but the ground colour is almost white. In both sexes the fringes and antennae are pink. This species may be confused with the female form *helice* of the Clouded Yellow, particularly on the underside, but in *hyale* the black margin on the forewing upper side does not extend round the lower corner as it does in *croceus*.

The Pale Clouded Yellow is common in Europe, but rare in this country, although in favourable years small numbers may reach our southern coasts. Specimens have been reported during the months from May to September. Its habits and haunts are similar to those of the Clouded Yellow and the larval foodplants are clover spp., lucerne (*Medicago sativa*), and bird's foot trefoil (*Lotus corniculatus*).

Pale Clouded Yellow: upper sides – ♂ *above*, ♀ *below*; wingspan 52 mm.

Pieridae Berger's Clouded Yellow – *Colias australis* (Verity)

This is almost identical in appearance to the Pale Clouded Yellow, the most noticeable difference being the reduced black border on the hindwing of *australis*. Since there is a certain amount of normal variation between individuals of both species, other points of difference are not reliable.

The butterfly occurs in France, Germany, Spain, and Portugal. In flight it is impossible to distinguish it from *hyale*, but it tends to favour chalk hills and downland where the larval foodplants grow. These are horse-shoe vetch (*Hippocrepis comosa*) and crown vetch (*Coronilla varia*). Migrants normally arrive in the southern counties of England in June, but are very rare. Before 1947 this was thought to be a subspecies of *hyale*, but in that year L. A. Berger determined that it was a separate species – in fact the larvae of the two are totally different in appearance, and have different foodplants.

Berger's Clouded Yellow: ♂ underside; wingspan 52 mm

Berger's Clouded Yellow: ♀ underside

Glossary

Abdomen Third major division of the body.

Aberration A butterfly which differs in appearance from the normal.

Androconia The scent scales of the male butterfly.

Antenna One of a pair of sensory organs on the front of the head; the tip is clubbed.

Apex The tip of the forewing.

Cell The space in the centre of the wing enclosed by veins.

Chitin Horny material comprising the external skeleton.

Chorion The eggshell.

Class A division of a phylum.

Costa The leading edge of the wing.

Coxa The basal segment of a leg.

Cremaster A device, often bearing hooks, on the last segment of the pupa, enabling it to attach itself to a silk pad.

Crepuscular Flying at dusk.

Cuticle The outer skin or casing.

Dimorphism Occurring in two distinct forms.

Dorsal Upper surface.

Ecdysis Moulting; the shedding of the larval skin.

Family A group of closely related genera.

Femur The third segment of a leg.

Frass Larval faeces.

Frenulum Wing-coupling apparatus in moths, consisting of a bristle on the leading edge of the hindwing at the base, which locks on to the forewing.

Ganglia groups of neurons.

Genus A group of closely allied species.

Gynandromorph A butterfly exhibiting male and female colour and marking.

Haemolymph The blood of insects.

Heterocera Sub-order of the Lepidoptera comprising the moths.

Imago The adult butterfly.

Instar The period between two larval moults.

Lateral On the sides.

Lepidoptera Order of insects including butterflies and moths.

Lunule A crescent-shaped marking.

Malphigian tubes Excretory system in insects.

Mandibles Jaws.

Metamorphosis The four stages of development of a butterfly – egg, larva, pupa, imago.

Micropyle The tiny opening at the top of the egg through which the sperm passes to fertilize it.

Mosaic A butterfly with patchy characteristics of the opposite sex.

Neurons Nerve fibres.

Order A division of a class.

Osmeterium Pair of horns behind the head of certain larvae giving off unpleasant smell.

Palpi Sensory organs in front of the face of the butterfly.

Phylum A major group in the classification of the Animal Kingdom.

Proboscis The tubular tongue of the butterfly, through which it feeds.

Prolegs The abdominal legs, and chief means of locomotion, of the larva.

Rhopalocera Sub-order of the Lepidoptera comprising the butterflies.

Species A group of closely related individuals capable of interbreeding.

Spinnerets Tubes from which silk is extruded by the larva.

Spiracles The external openings of the tracheae.

Tarsus Foot.

Thorax The second major division of the butterfly's body, bearing the legs and wings.

Tibia The fourth segment of a leg.

Tracheae Respiratory tubes.

Trochanter Second segment of a leg.

Tubercle A small projection on the skin of a larva which often bears spines.

Ventral Lower surface.

♂ male

♀ female

Index

English Names

Adonis Blue, 98–9

Bath White, 155
Berger's Clouded Yellow, 156
Black Hairstreak, 116–17
Black-veined White, 155
Brimstone, 130–1
Brown Argus, 90–1
Brown Hairstreak, 110–11

Camberwell Beauty, 153
Chalkhill Blue, 96–7
Chequered Skipper, 138–41
Clouded Yellow, 128–9
Comma, 78–9
Common Blue, 94–5

Dark Green Fritillary, 56–7
Dingy Skipper, 134–5
Duke of Burgundy Fritillary, 84–5

Essex Skipper, 144–5

Gatekeeper, 44–5
Glanville Fritillary, 64–5
Grayling, 40–1
Green Hairstreak, 108–9
Green-veined White, 124–5
Grizzled Skipper, 136–7

Heath Fritillary, 66–7
Hedge Brown, 44–5
High Brown Fritillary, 58–9
Holly Blue, 102–3

Large Blue, 100–1
Large Copper, 106–7
Large Heath, 48–9
Large Skipper, 150–1
Large Tortoiseshell, 74–5
Large White, 120–1
Long-tailed Blue, 153
Lulworth Skipper, 146–7

Marbled White, 38–9
Marsh Fritillary, 62–3
Mazarine Blue, 154
Meadow Brown, 42–3
Milkweed, 152
Monarch, 152

Northern Brown Argus, 92–3

Orange Tip, 126–7

Painted Lady, 70–1

Pale Clouded Yellow, 156
Peacock, 76–7
Pearl-bordered Fritillary, 52–3
Purple Emperor, 80–1
Purple Hairstreak, 112–13

Queen of Spain Fritillary, 152

Red Admiral, 68–9
Ringlet, 50–1

Scotch Argus, 36–7
Short-tailed Blue, 154
Silver-spotted Skipper, 148–9
Silver-studded Blue, 88–9
Silver-washed Fritillary, 60–1
Small Blue, 86–7
Small Copper, 104–5
Small Heath, 46–7
Small Mountain Ringlet, 34–5
Small Pearl-bordered Fritillary, 54–5
Small Skipper, 142–3
Small Tortoiseshell, 72–3
Small White, 122–3
Speckled Wood, 30–1
Swallowtail, 132–3

Wall, 32–3
White Admiral, 82–3
White Letter Hairstreak, 114–15
Wood White 118–19

·

Scientific Names

Subspecies, aberrations and forms are listed under the full scientific name only. Ab. – aberration; f. – form.

acteon, Thymelicus, 146–7
aegeria, Pararge, 30–1
aethiops, Erebia, 36–7
agestis, Aricia, 90–1
Aglais urticae, 72–3
aglaja, Argynnis, 56–7
Anthocharis cardamines, 126–7
—cardamines hibernica, 126
antiopa, Nymphalis, 153
Apatura iris, 80–1
—iris ab. iole, 80
Aphantopus hyperantus, 50–1
—hyperantus ab. lanceolata, 50
—hyperantus ab. obsoleta, 50
Aporia crataegi, 155
argiades, Everes, 154
argiolus, Celastrina, 102–3

argus, Plebejus, 88–9
Argynnis aglaja, 56–7
—aglaja scotica, 56
—cydippe, 58–9
—lathonia, 152
—paphia, 60–1
—paphia f. valezina, 60–1
Aricia agestis, 90–1
—artaxerxes, 92–3
—artaxerxes salmacis, 92
arion, Maculinea, 100–1
artaxerxes, Aricia, 92–3
atalanta, Vanessa, 68–9
athalia, Mellicta, 66–7
aurinia, Euphydryas, 62–3
australis, Colias, 156

bellargus, Lysandra, 98–9
betulae, Thecla, 110–11
boeticus, Lampides, 153
Boloria euphrosyne, 52–3
—selene, 54–5
brassicae, Pieris, 120–1

c-album, Polygonia, 78–9
Callophrys rubi, 108–9
camilla, Ladoga, 82–3
cardamines, Anthocharis, 126–7
cardui, Vanessa, 70–1
Carterocephalus palaemon, 138–41
Celastrina argiolus, 102–3
cinxia, Melitaea, 64–5
Coenonympha pamphilus, 46–7
—tullia, 48–9
—tullia davus, 48
—tullia laidion, see scotica
—tullia philoxenus, see davus
—tullia polydama, 48
—tullia scotica, 48
—tullia tiphon, see polydama
Colias australis, 156
—croceus, 128–9
—croceus f. helice, 128–9
—hyale, 156
comma, Hesperia, 148–9
coridon, Lysandra, 96–7
crataegi, Aporia, 155
croceus, Colias, 128–9
Cupido minimus, 86–7
Cyaniris semiargus, 154
cydippe, Argynnis, 58–9

Danaus plexippus, 152
daplidice, Pontia, 155
dispar batavus, Lycaena, 106–7

epiphron, Erebia, 34–5
Erebia aethiops, 36–7

—epiphron, 34–5
Erynnis tages, 134–5
—tages baynesi, 134
euphrosyne, Boloria, 52–3
Euphydryas aurinia, 62–3
—aurinia anglicana, 62
—aurinia hibernica, 62
—aurinia scotica, 62
Everes argiades, 154

galathea, Melanargia, 38–9
Gonepteryx rhamni, 130–1

Hamearis lucina, 84–5
Hesperia comma, 148–9
Hipparchia semele, 40–1
—semele clarensis, 40
—semele hibernica, 40
—semele scota, 40
—semele thyone, 40
yale, Colias, 156
hyperantus, Aphantopus, 50–1

icarus, Polyommatus, 94–5
Inachis io, 76–7
o, Inachis, 76–7
iris, Apatura, 80–1

jurtina, Maniola, 42–3

Ladoga camilla, 82–3
Lampides boeticus, 153
Lasiommata megera, 32–3
lathonia, Argynnis, 152
Leptidea sinapis, 118–19
lineola, Thymelicus, 144–5
Lycaena dispar batavus, 106–7
—dispar dispar, 106
—dispar rutilus, 106
—phlaeas, 104–5
—phlaeas ab. caeruleopunctata, 104
Lysandra bellargus, 98–9

—bellargus ab. ceronus, 98
—coridon, 96–7
—coridon ab. fowleri, 96
—coridon ab. syngrapha, 96
—coridon ab. semisyngrapha, 96
lucina, Hamearis, 84–5

machaon, Papilio, 132–3
Maculinea arion, 100–1
malvae, Pyrgus, 136–7
Maniola jurtina, 42–3
—jurtina cassiteridum, 42
—jurtina iernes, 42
—jurtina insularis, 42
—jurtina splendida, 42
megera, Lasiommata, 32–3
Melanargia galathea, 38–9
Melitaea cinxia, 64–5
Mellicta athalia, 66–7
minimus, Cupido, 86–7

napi, Pieris, 124–5
Nymphalis antiopa, 153
—polychloros, 74–5

Ochlodes venata, 150–1

palaemon, Carterocephalus, 138–41
pamphilus, Coenonympha, 46–7
paphia, Argynnis, 60–1
Papilio machaon, 132–3
—machaon britannicus, 132
Pararge aegeria, 30–1
phlaeas, Lycaena, 104–5
Pieris brassicae, 120–1
—napi, 124–5
—napi britannica, 124
—rapae, 122–3
Plebejus argus, 88–9
—argus argus, 88
—argus caernensis, 88
—argus cretaceus, 88
—argus masseyi, 88

plexippus, Danaus, 152
polychloros, Nymphalis, 74–5
Polygonia c-album, 78–9
—c-album f. hutchinsoni, 78–9
Polyommatus icarus, 94–5
Pontia daplidice, 155
pruni, Strymonidia, 116–17
Pyrgus malvae, 136–7
Pyronia tithonus, 44–5

quercus, Quercusia, 112–13
Quercusia quercus, 112–13
—quercus ab. flavimaculatus, 112

rapae, Pieris, 122–3
rhamni, Gonepteryx, 130–1
rubi, Callophrys, 108–9

selene, Boloria, 54–5
semele, Hipparchia, 40–1
semiargus, Cyaniris, 154
sinapis, Leptidea, 118–19
Strymonidia pruni, 116–17
—w-album, 114–15
sylvestris, Thymelicus, 142–3

tages, Erynnis, 134–5
Thecla betulae, 110–11
Thymelicus acteon, 146–7
—lineola, 144–5
—sylvestris, 142–3
tithonus, Pyronia, 44–5
tullia, Coenonympha, 48–9

urticae, Aglais, 72–3

Vanessa atalanta, 68–9
—cardui, 70–1
venata, Ochlodes, 150–1

w-album, Strymonidia, 114–15